KU-265-712

Mentoring Executives and Directors

David Clutterbuck and David Megginson

ELSEVIER
BUTTERWORTH
HEINEMANN

AMSTERDAM • BOSTON • HEIDELBERG • LONDON • NEW YORK • OXFORD
PARIS • SAN DIEGO • SAN FRANCISCO • SINGAPORE • SYDNEY • TOKYO

Elsevier Butterworth Heinemann
Linacre House, Jordan Hill, Oxford OX2 8DP
200 Wheeler Road, Burlington, MA 01803

First published 1999
Reprinted 2000
Transferred to digital printing 2004

Copyright © 1999, David Clutterbuck and David Megginson. All rights reserved

The right of David Clutterbuck and David Megginson to be identified as the
authors of this work has been asserted in accordance with the Copyright,
Designs and Patents Act 1988

No part of this publication may be reproduced in any material form (including
photocopying or storing in any medium by electronic means and whether
or not transiently or incidentally to some other use of this publication) without
the written permission of the copyright holder except in accordance with the
provisions of the Copyright, Designs and Patents Act 1988 or under the terms of
a licence issued by the Copyright Licensing Agency Ltd, 90 Tottenham Court Road,
London, England WIT 4LP. Applications for the copyright holder's written
permission to reproduce any part of this publication should be addressed
to the publisher

Permissions may be sought directly from Elsevier's Science & Technology Rights
Department in Oxford, UK: phone: (+44) 1865 843830, fax: (+44) 1865 853333,
e-mail: permissions@elsevier.co.uk. You may also complete your request on-line via
the Elsevier homepage (http://www.elsevier.com), by selecting 'Customer Support'
and then 'Obtaining Permissions'

British Library Cataloguing in Publication Data
A catalogue record for this book is available from the British Library

ISBN 0 7506 3695 5

For information on all Elsevier Butterworth-Heinemann
publications visit our website at www.bh.com

Printed and bound in Great Britain by Lightning Source UK Ltd

CENTRE	Lincoln
CHECKED	PS
ZONE	Maune
CLASS MARK / SUFFIX	658.312 ChU
LOAN PERIOD	1 month

Contents

Part 1

Every executive needs a mentor

Why this book?

Mentoring Executives and Directors is the direct result of the explosion in mentoring at the top of organizations in recent years. Relatively little study has been made of how executives find and use mentors, neither on their rise to senior positions and when they get there; nor on how executives become mentors in turn.

What research literature there is tends to view mentoring as primarily a vehicle for sponsorship rather than development. Typical of this view is the study undertaken by Tilton Willcox in the 1980s (Willcox, 1987) who found that more than half of 250 executives considered that some form of top management sponsorship was essential or important in reaching an executive post. Willcox also concluded that high level mentors 'significantly influenced [executives'] advancement to [their] current rank' and that 'organizational politics play an important role in promotion' in their organizations.

Classic studies from the United States (Levinson, 1978) also suggest a strong correlation between finding a mentor at a junior level in the organization and achieving top jobs.

It is notable that almost all these studies involve executives *looking back* on their careers and registering gratitude to mentors who helped them up the lower rungs of the ladder. Very few talk about the mentors they have now. This may be partly because it is not considered macho to admit you need help when you are at the top. Whatever the reason, the lack of open discussion around this topic is one of the main reasons for researching and writing this book.

In defining our topic, the first step is to reach an understanding of what we mean by mentoring and in particular the mentoring of executives and directors. The definition of mentoring which we established in *Mentoring in Action* (Megginson and Clutterbuck,1995) is:

> Off-line help by one person to another in making significant transitions in knowledge, work or thinking.

The same definition applies to the mentoring of executives and directors. We would argue that the frequency of the significant transitions required to deal with a changing environment are, if anything, greater for the most senior managers than for anyone else in the organization.

Development is different

One of the themes that will emerge again and again in this book is embodied in the words 'significant transitions' in the above definition.

Mentoring supports a process that is about enabling and supporting – sometimes triggering – major change in people's life and work. As such it is about developing the whole person, rather than training in particular skills. Our development through life can be seen as like a graph which rises as we increase in competence and confidence. However, the slope of the graph changes from time to time. There are sharp rises, as well as relatively level plateaux. Mentoring is especially valuable during these periods of rapid change.

It is like climbing the side of a mountain. While we are struggling up the steep bits we are breathless, challenged, single-minded, and in need of some support and sustenance. Technically there may be some moves that we can only make roped up to someone else. It is here that the mentoring process comes into its own. Coaching can help us move along the relatively level ground to the next big challenge. When we face a cliff we need help that will enable us to exercise new skills, new strategies, new perspectives.

Mentoring can help with this change and enable the developing executive or director to get to the higher ground where they can have a quite different perspective. They will see further mountain ranges, new ways forward, which were simply not imaginable from the plateau below. This means that mentoring needs to be a process which encourages new perspectives, changed ways of thinking, deeper self-knowledge. These transitions are usually irreversible, in the sense that once the insight is gained it cannot be lost again. It may be set on one side under the pressure of events, but it will be there, working away on the executive to shape their future behaviour. It is this change in perspective that makes mentoring such a powerful intervention, and it is the dynamics of personal reflective space (PRS) that makes this power manifest. Later in this chapter we will explore this space and how the mentor and the executive or director they are helping can use it.

Curtain raisers for mentoring

En route to the top, key issues for mentees appear to be:

- How do I make myself noticed?
- How do I get the experience that will enhance my career prospects?
- How do I gain sufficient understanding of what happens at more senior levels?
- How do I learn to manage business politics?
- How do I get myself assigned to the 'right' projects?
- How do I create the influence and information networks that will enable me to operate effectively at a senior level?

- How do I develop the depth of self-awareness necessary to operate at that level?

Once they get to an executive position, a whole new series of issues emerges:
- How do I continue to learn when most of the knowledge I need to acquire is intuitively based?
- How do I stimulate constructive challenge from my peers and people below me in the organizational structure?
- How do I cope with the stress of my responsibilities? (This concern seems to come earlier and earlier in people's careers.)
- How can I manage my performance better, when it is so much more difficult to measure my contribution?
- How can I develop other people, when I have less and less hands-on time with them?
- How do I achieve through influence rather than command?
- Who can I test ideas out on without raising fears or expectations?
- Do I have sufficient self-mastery to continue to grow with the job?
- How do I manage my personal credibility within the organization?

If the person is also a director, new issues include:
- How do I learn how to distinguish between my roles as senior function head and director?
- How do I develop the skills to become a chief executive or a non-executive director?
- How can I and my colleagues work together in 'collaborative independence'?
- How do I ensure I know what is really going on in the organization?
- Am I providing an effective role model for the values the top team espouses? Could I do better?
- Is my strategic thinking sufficiently broad to contribute effectively to the process of creating and interpreting the business vision?
- Do I have sufficient contextual understanding of disciplines I have little hands-on experience in?
- What am I going to do with my life/career from now on?

These themes will occur and recur throughout the course of this book, which has been designed firstly to stimulate debate about the nature and objectives of mentoring, and secondly to explore the experience of mentoring at senior levels from a variety of perspectives – mentor, mentee, scheme co-ordinator (where the mentoring takes place as part of a formal scheme) and interested observer.

In preparing this book we have assembled over twenty cases of executive mentoring. Our analysis of these cases has, of course, been grounded on our own experience and preconceptions about how executive mentoring works. The models, frameworks and assumptions that we use in this work are the subject of the rest of this first part of the book. Part 2 is made up of the cases, which are organized into three sections – private sector, public sector and voluntary sector. Many of these cases we have prepared ourselves from interviews carried out specifically for this book. We have also included other voices to enrich the data we have available to you, the reader. We have invited researchers to talk about mentoring that they have conducted (A1 Durham University's small business schemes) or that they have observed as outsiders (A2 Liz Borredon's account of a French mentor, A10 Lida Beers' story of a peer mentoring in the Netherlands, B7 Richard Hale's reading of the mentoring of a health trust's finance director). We have asked scheme organizers to talk about their own schemes (A5 Carl Eric Gestberg's scheme in ABB Sweden, A7 Nick Holley's approach in Lex, A11 Trude Stolpe's account of mentoring in Axel Johnsson, Sweden, A13 Nina Lazeron's report of her HRM Director's mentoring experience in Heineken, the Netherlands), and professional mentors tell their own stories (A3 James Cannon, B4 and C2 Judy Weleminski's account of relationships in the public and voluntary sector respectively). We have in two cases separate accounts of the same relationship (A8 Colin Palmer mentoring Nigel Harrison, B1 Ian Flemming mentoring Julia Essex). In this way we have increased the diversity of the accounts you will read in the second part of this book. Of course, even the interviews we have conducted ourselves show colossal differences based on the different focus, temperament or context of the people whose stories we share through the mentoring process. In the interviews we have kept as closely as we can to the interviewee's own words, ad we have checked our text with our respondents. Those who are familiar with transcribing talk will know that people – even the very articulate people who are the subjects of our research – do not talk in sentences! So we have amended the accounts to increase the ease of readability of what they have to say.

In Part 3 we bring together the sense that we have made of this multiplicity of stories. Again we keep the interpretations open by building in perspectives of others. We have been greatly helped by participants in the seminars we have run while preparing this text – who have read some of our cases and offered their readings of their significance. In particular we are grateful to three of our respondents who spent a day with us working through a large number of the cases and coming to their own views of the issues that emerge. Their wisdom and incisiveness have shaped the issues that we address in Part 3 though, of course, any opinions which we express are our own.

Some of the issues which struck our co-researchers were:

- The qualities of executive mentors: wisdom, outside experience, good questions and listening, role modelling, credibility, patience, networking, help in 'becoming oneself', two-way insight, balancing process and content, being dependable, helping manage knowledge.
- The nature of executive mentoring relationships: triggered by crisis, long-term very high trust needed, crucial for overcoming isolation, the chemistry being right is essential, differing bases for respect, planning and preparation by both parties.
- Organizational issues: integral to organization development, need for an underlying model of mentoring, link to organizational models (balanced scorecard, transformation, EFQM, etc.), need for a systematic approach overall.
- Patterns in national approaches to mentoring – northern Europe: non-selective (available for whole cohort), scheme-based, egalitarian, strongly mutual; UK: individualistic, career questions and life balance issues predominate; France and southern Europe: few stories, formality of relations between managers a barrier; US: sponsorship and promoting careers are more readily accepted than in Europe.
- Pattern of purpose by sector – public sector: linked to course and career; private sector: linked to balanced lives and performance; voluntary sector: values shared learning across sectors.

Lonely at the top

The metaphor of the Captain of the ship has dominated thinking about managerial leadership for far too long. The Captain stands alone, unguided, unbowed, the master of a small, enclosed world. His word is the law and it is his defiance of the elements, his skill at direction that steer the vessel away from danger and result in rapid, safe passage. *Mutiny on the Bounty* and many other tales explore what happens to those who dare to tell the Captain he is wrong.

The problem for the Captain is that he or she has no-one to turn to – for advice, for acquiring learning, for questioning assumptions and behaviours. Once seafarers became Captains, it was assumed (whatever the reality) that they had no further need to learn, or to be given encouragement and support. The same principle applied to the next couple of ranks down – the more senior you were, the less learning and support you needed.

The analogy with the modern CEO and business executives fails on a number of counts. Firstly, the CEO's word is not law, nor is the ship of business an isolated small world. It has to answer to a variety of often vocal stakeholders. Secondly, executive directors are expected to operate as a team (as opposed to the Board as a whole, which is a very different animal, especially when it includes non-executive directors). Increasingly, this means sharing knowledge and learning, leveraging each other's strengths and compensating for each other's weaknesses. Thirdly, no-one is capable of understanding everything that is going on in an organization, unless it is very small. And fourthly, top managers are increasingly having to accept that learning does not stop when you reach the executive suite – far from it, indeed, for that is one of the occasions within a career when learning has to accelerate. (Others include the first job and the first managerial role.) It takes courage to declare, as recently did the chief executive of one of Europe's largest construction groups, that tomorrow's Board will have to have a very different, more comprehensive set of skills than the present incumbents. Such a statement focuses the minds of the top team on what has to be done to develop executive talent, so that the next Board will be home-grown.

Companies that have abandoned the myth of the CEO as Captain of the ship open up a whole variety of developmental options, both for the individual executive directors and for the top team as a whole. As a group, top teams and boards are more and more making effective use of approaches such as action learning (Casey, 1993) to facilitate the process of learning from and about each other. Externally facilitated decision-making is increasingly common, valued because it combines exploration and extrapolation with urgently needed practical outcomes. Business schools are booming with executive short courses, many of them customized to the learning needs of particular companies.

Personal reflective space

The missing ingredient in most of this activity is frequently *personal reflective space* (PRS). PRS can be defined as 'the seized opportunity to develop personal insight through uninterrupted and purposeful reflective activity'. Note some of the words used here. The *opportunity* has to be *seized* to be useful – not always easy in a busy executive schedule. Personal *insight* is a critical ingredient in effecting significant purposeful personal change. *Uninterrupted and purposeful* means what it says. The individual needs to find sufficient quiet time to think issues through, explore their 'inner meaning' and to analyse and compare different strategies. For most people, that means at least an hour.

Research indicates that directors find it very hard to reflect. Alan Mumford *et al.* (1990) explored the learning styles of over 100 directors and classified them into one of Mumford's four styles of learner (activist, reflector, theorist and pragmatist). Of the four styles, reflectors were by far the smallest group.

Rather like dreaming, quality reflective time allows the learner to pass through several layers and rhythms. The first phase can be described as *disaggregated*. The executive is still in his or her normal working state, high on activity (in both senses of the phrase). The emphasis of his or her thinking is primarily on *what* needs to be done, and *how*, rather than on *why*; and on the urgent rather than the important.

The second phase can be called *acknowledgment* or *framing*. The reflector has been aware of an issue that needs to be addressed, but has not previously articulated it in a coherent way. Framing involves putting an initial definition or structure to the issue, some clear boundaries as to what it is and is not, as an essential first step to dealing with it. It is the complexity of the framing process that prevents us from doing it 'on the hoof' and that complexity arises as much, if not usually more, from the need to apply values and emotional understanding to an issue than to difficulty in understanding the rational and/or logistical aspects of it.

The third phase is one of *implication analysis*. What does it imply if I don't deal with this issue? If I do? What am I afraid of? What is the best or worst that could happen? What do I want to happen? Why? This kind of thought process is often an essential precursor to the next phase, *insight*.

Insight is the recognition of a deeper level of understanding. It can be a 'truth' – perhaps a statement about one's behaviour, personality or motivations that had not previously been apparent; or a perception of a pattern or structure to events or data that had previously seemed random; or a significant new perception, such as viewing a persistent problem as an opportunity. Insight can also involve a deeper sense of what one's purpose is. This can be a narrow purpose in relation to the issue being considered, or a wider life purpose, which becomes clearer from examining the focused issue in this reflective way.

Phase five is about *reframing*. The individual revisits the issue(s) in the light of the insight gained. This enables them to draw upon logic and emotion to develop a set of options or alternatives for dealing with the issues. A frequent outcome is the aggregation of a number of smaller, apparently intractable problems into one or two larger ones that have a much clearer set of choices attached to them. These choices form the sixth phase, considering and selecting between options.

It is typical, watching someone go through these phases, to see their physical energy dampen, the more reflective they become. Physical energy hits nadir at insight level, gradually building up again as the executive begins to perceive viable actions he or she can take. Visualizing

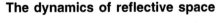

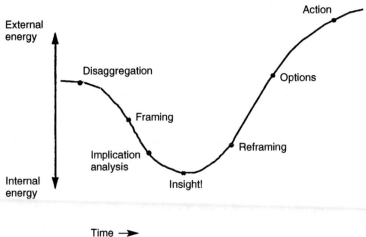

Figure 1.1 A model of personal reflective space

those actions releases more and more energy until they are back into their normal working state, itching to make things happen.

Reflective activity, the final part of the definition, might seem to contradict this picture of energy flow. But we have noticed that, to maximize mental activity, it is generally beneficial for a short time to minimize physical activity. True, some people (including one of the authors) often seem to think most creatively when they walk around, but they are almost always in reframing or options mode when they do so.

Reflection also implies, in its natural sciences definition, some form of interaction. It is the movement of light that makes a mirror work. For the individual taking time out to ponder, reflection can be seen as a dialogue with oneself. Nonetheless, it *is* a dialogue.

That dialogue can be much more powerful, if it is carried out with someone else, who has the skills not only to ask the questions you would ask yourself, but also those you would not ask yourself. **That person is a mentor.**

Why the rise of interest in executive mentoring?

Wise CEOs and directors have sought counsel and reassurance from sources outside their organizations since organizations began. The term mentor originates in Greek mythology, but the practice of mentoring dates from much earlier. There is increasing evidence that the gradual dominance of Homo Hominis (Modern Man) over other related species was a consequence of becoming more and more competent at passing knowledge and wisdom from generation to generation.

In recent years, there has been a remarkable surge in director and executive mentoring. There are several reasons for this:

- Jobs at the top involve increasing pressure – on time, to demonstrate performance, to meet the often conflicting demands of different stakeholders. The risks of being an executive or director grow each year, along with the volume of legislation from national or supranational sources. Maintaining a sense of balance on a multitude of complex issues is very difficult if the people you discuss them with are all involved as you are. It makes a great deal of sense to seek the perspective of an unbiased, trustworthy individual, whose judgement you value.
- Maintaining the balance between work and home has become much more difficult. With allowance made for commuting time and working at home, . today's typical executive works at least as long hours as his or her Victorian counterpart, who had a 60 hour week. Early retirement is as much a symptom of exhaustion as seizing the opportunity created by individuals' greater wealth. Reflective dialogue about how to maintain a quality of personal life are more often than not a feature of mentoring relationships at this level.
- As executives face up to their own needs for continuous performance improvement, they need to gain greater insight into their motivations, their strengths and weaknesses, particularly in how they relate to other people in the business. Admitting a lack of confidence can be very difficult inside the organization, yet fairly easy to an experienced listener from outside. Good mentors help executives understand their behaviours, identify where to build on good habits and address destructive ones, and plan personal improvement.
- Flatter hierarchies make the jump from one level of management to another increasingly difficult. In particular, the transitions between specialist and general manager, between executive and director, and between director and chief executive all involve radical changes in the way the individual makes judgements and manages his or her team. It helps greatly to have the support and guidance of someone who has been through the same experience and is able to make their experiences relevant to you. In a recent research project examining high performance companies around the world (Goldsmith and Clutterbuck, 1997), one of the common characteristics was that the outgoing CEO always remained in some capacity to act as mentor to the new CEO, until he or she no longer needed the support.

- The expectation that executives would pursue careers within a single organization has largely vanished. Career planning has become an essential activity for the ambitious executive, providing a role for the mentor who is able to help the person think through choices and suggest new avenues to explore. Here are three summaries of issues raised in mentoring sessions with one of the authors by different CEOs over less than a month:

  > My contract comes to an end in two years. I could renew it, but do I want to carry on doing what I'm doing now? (Discussion revealed that, in order to change careers in two years' time, the executive needed to start creating opportunities now.)

  > I'm only in this post for a year, until a new appointment is made. I've decided not to put my hat in the ring – I want a less high pressure job where I can spend more time with my family.

  > I've reached the top here. The next logical step is to European headquarters, but my family have already made too many sacrifices for my job. I won't put them through a move abroad as well.

- Small business enterprises have become an almost obsessive interest for successive governments across Europe. The problem is that, as the seedcorn for tomorrow's successful giants, a great many get eaten or wither before they can take root properly. A major cause of the high failure rate is that the owner-managers are so busy growing the business that they do not grow their own abilities in tandem. As a result, they rapidly outreach their competence. Small business counsellors can help to grow the business, but it often needs a mentor to help the entrepreneur plan and manage his or her own development.

Formal versus informal mentoring

To some extent mentoring at senior management level is always informal. A more meaningful distinction might be between paid and unpaid mentoring, or between peer and professional mentoring.

Executive coaching (which is often confusingly described as mentoring by consultants trying to take their product upmarket) has to be relatively formal. It starts with an assumption that the executive needs to make significant improvements in a specific area of behaviour, skills or knowledge. It tends to have a strong element of judgement by the coach, who gives feedback about what he or she observes.

By contrast, mentoring tends to be much more holistic. It uses many of the same techniques, but concentrates on helping the executive gain his or her own insights. It encompasses a much wider range of potential issues for discussion. Whereas the coach uses his or her experience to guide the executive along a particular track, the effective mentor allows the learner to manage the process of drawing down on the mentor's experience.

Of course, mentoring relationships often shade into coaching and vice versa. Does it really matter what you call it, if it works for the individual? But the distinction between the two processes is more than academic. Current research into 'helping to learn' roles suggests strongly that clarity of expectation about the role makes a significant difference to the quality of the outcomes (Clutterbuck, 1998).

Informal mentoring has historically been the norm for executives and directors. It usually starts at an early stage in people's careers. A study of women in business by one of the authors (Clutterbuck and Devine, 1987) found that a high proportion of female executives perceived that a mentor had been significant in giving them the confidence and self-image to seek advancement, in making them visible to top management and in helping them learn how to handle organizational politics. In very few cases were these relationships formal.

Formal (paid, professional) mentoring is undoubtedly on the increase. Why this should be so is not immediately clear, but reasons advanced include:

- the difficulty of finding people with the *breadth* of relevant experience to meet the needs of a would-be top management mentee
- the recognition by executives, especially CEOs, that this has to be *quality time* if they are to get the maximum benefit out of it. That implies that the mentor should have a higher level of behavioural skills and insight than most senior managers have time to acquire
- greater acceptance of the role of professional help for individuals and teams in business – career counselling, process consultancy, personality profiling and so on.

What qualifies someone to be a professional mentor is also still debatable. The UK has a BTEC qualification and plans for a National Vocational Qualification in mentoring at three levels, of which the highest may be 'professional' mentor.

A further senior executive mentoring role that lies somewhere between the formal and informal is the increasingly common practice whereby the retiring CEO becomes a chairperson/mentor to his or her successor. The transition between director and CEO requires a period of rapid personal growth if the new CEO is to avoid expensive mistakes, both for the organization and for himself or herself as an individual. Having the retired CEO around as chairman for a period provides a very useful sounding board and source of cautionary advice. Of course, the chairman acting in this role has to have the strong respect of the new CEO and the CEO in turn has to have a strong inclination to listen and learn ... which is not always the case.

What do executive mentors do?

As illustrated in the cases within this book, executive mentors play a full range of roles, often within the same relationship. Among the most common are:

- Sounding board: someone independent and uninvolved, who can give honest feedback on how the executive plans to tackle an issue. Implicit in the role of sounding board is that the executive respects both the mentor's accumulated experience and his or her ability to recognize when and how to draw on that experience – in short, the mentor's *wisdom*. Examples of sounding boards within our case studies include.... See A2 and A8.
- Critical friend: someone willing and able to 'speak truth to power', to say openly the things that colleagues are reluctant to expose, either from embarrassment, fear, politeness or (occasionally) malice. The critical friend provides a source of challenge to the executive's assumptions, probing beneath the surface of issues to test the logic of decisions, prompting the executive to question his and others' behaviour and motivations. Examples of critical friends in our cases include.... See B1 and C1.
- Listener: someone who is simply there to offer encouragement and provide a listening ear. See A10 and B5.
- Counsellor: an empathetic listener, with the reflective and questioning skills to help the executive analyse problems and opportunities in a dispassionate manner. Effective counsellor mentors do not ignore the emotional side of issues under discussion, however. Rather, they help executives explore how their emotional drives affect their apparently rational decisions. They can help the executive increase his or her resilience to change, and manage areas of weakness either by coming to terms with them and finding ways to compensate, or by planning significant changes in behaviour. They are particularly adept at helping the executive identify and respond to repetitive dysfunctional behaviour. See A2 and A3.
- Career advisor: helping the executive think through career options, plan personal development towards defined career goals and learn lessons from previous career experience. See A1 and B4.
- Networker: providing access to networks the executive will find useful in both career and developmental terms. See A1 and B3.
- Coach: helping the executive make personal change happen, especially at the behavioural level. A coaching approach is most likely to be of benefit

when the person has a specific behavioural issue to tackle, or needs to demonstrate a specific interpersonal competence, over a relatively short period of time. See A9 and A12.

In a study conducted by one of the authors several years ago (Clutterbuck, 1993) over 100 mentoring pairs were established for newly created Boards of National Health Trusts in the UK, within the Oxford Regional Health Authority. Mentors and mentees were closely agreed on the most valuable roles: sounding board, critical friend and listener. (Mentors also felt they played a strong role as 'giver of encouragement' although the executives recognized this much less.) It would not be a valid conclusion to assume that all executive mentoring relationships would have the same core roles – the relationships were established for a very precise purpose (developing personal development plans) and for a very specific type of Board. However, it *is* significant that the roles most valued by executive mentees tended to be the more reflective options.

Three common roles

Wider discussions with executives about their mentors suggest that they seek help from people prepared (or able) to play one of three largely distinctive and often incompatible roles. For simplicity's sake, we call these *executive coach, elder statesperson* and *reflective mentor*.

The executive coach is usually part of a short-term relationship, based on a clearly defined skills or behavioural issue for the executive concerned. Some coaches shadow the executive closely for a period, to observe what they do and provide objective feedback. Executive coaches need strong observation and communication skills, but often may not have had significant personal experience of managing at the top.

Executives tend to seek them out (or have coaches thrust upon them) when they:

- are deeply concerned about some aspect of their performance
- want to make some specific changes in behaviour
- want to acquire some specific skills.

The elder statesperson is typically a senior player who has 'been there, seen it, done it'. Elder statespersons give the benefit of their experience and may act as role models. They need good listening skills and the ability to withhold judgement and advice until it is needed. This can be very frustrating for the person who is itching to pass on their accumulated wisdom and many of these characters spoil the role by trying to give more than is wanted. In doing so, they risk taking the ownership of the relationship away from the mentee. Elder statespersons tend also to be very well networked and able to introduce the executive to new sources of information and influence. If the relationship works well, it often leads to an enduring friendship.

Executives tend to seek elder statespersons when they:

- want a successful role model to follow
- simply need a sounding board
- want to tap into a source of much greater experience, without using consultants (e.g. a CEO making a first acquisition).

Reflective mentors operate at a more intensive, holistic level than either the coach or the elder statesperson. They help executives explore their own issues, build their own insights and self-awareness and develop their own unique ways of handling how they interact with key colleagues and the business. They use current issues to examine recurrent patterns of thinking and behaviour, asking penetrating questions and stimulating the executive to take control of issues s/he has avoided. They build the executive's confidence through greater self-understanding.

Executives seek reflective mentors when they:

- are keen to maintain the pace of their learning
- recognize the need for constructive challenge, beyond what they will receive from insiders and non-executives
- want to build and follow through demanding personal learning plans
- are committed to managing their own development and owning the processes involved
- want to explore a wide range of issues as they emerge and become important to them
- want to develop a more effective mentoring style in the way they develop others.

Most of the examples in this book refer to either the reflective mentor or elder statesperson roles. Of the two, effective reflective mentors are more difficult to find, because they require an unusual combination of attributes. In particular, they need:

- a broad exposure to executive decision-making and processes
- a large store of relevant business, strategic and behavioural models – and the capacity to generate other models on the spot, to help executives explore the context of issues under discussion
- strong interpersonal skills, typically underpinned with some competence in counselling.

This combination of skills enables the reflective mentor to deal with a very wide spread of business and personal issues and to adopt a variety of helping roles according to the executive's need. They may switch between coach, counsellor, networker, critical friend or sounding board all within the same session. (For a detailed view of this process within mentoring in general, see *Learning Alliances*; Clutterbuck, 1998.)

How reflective mentors approach the task

We mentioned earlier that energy levels are generally muted in reflective space. One of the reasons this is particularly so in executive mentoring is that the mentor deliberately helps the executive step outside the box of his or her job and personal circumstances, so they can look in at it together. It is like standing in front of the mirror with someone else, who can help you see things about you that have become too familiar for you to notice. However, there are times when mentoring sessions become very emotional, particularly at the framing, implication analysis and insight phases. Reflective space may be the only space in which people are able to release pent-up emotion, particularly where it relates to issues they have been avoiding, or which affect their sense of self. It is far from unusual to see an executive – male or female – break into tears as they relive a particularly frustrating episode in their current or previous work, or in their personal life. This release of energy – whether through anger, tears or intense physical activity – can often be a precursor to the calmness where insight occurs.

Mentoring and emotional intelligence

While the concept of emotional intelligence has been somewhat oversold, it nonetheless provides a neat and relatively practical way at looking at the range of competencies an executive needs to exhibit in order to be fully functional in the role. Given that over-reliance on some aspects of behavioural interaction with others may well have propelled the executive to senior levels in the first place, there may be a considerable amount of *emotional unlearning* to take place. The degree to which the executive is open to such learning – and the inevitable discomfort of discovery about oneself – will influence both the mentoring style and the benefit the executive can extract from the relationship.

Emotional intelligence, as defined by Goleman (1996) involves five key skills:

- knowing one's emotions (self-awareness)
- managing emotions (handling feelings)
- motivating oneself (marshalling emotions in the service of a goal)
- recognizing emotions in others (empathy)
- handling relationships (social competence).

One of the ways in which the executive mentor can help the executive build greater understanding and strength in each of these five areas is to ask penetrating questions, constantly pushing for insights. Some examples follow.

Knowing one's emotions
The mentor helps the executive separate the emotional and intellectual content of issues and develop an understanding of the interaction between the two. Typical questions:

- What exactly happened?
- What did you feel before, during and after?
- Why do you feel that way?
- Is there a pattern here?
- Do you think you might see this differently as an independent observer?
- How can you raise your real-time awareness of feelings?
- How do you feel about yourself? (What do you like/dislike about yourself?)
- How do you feel about the people you work with? (Do you like/respect/value them?)

Managing emotions
The mentor helps the executive develop greater control of feelings:

- Is the way you feel appropriate? Helpful?
- How do you think you should feel?
- How can you gain greater control over your emotions?
- How can you *use* emotion to achieve goals?
- When and how should you state to others what you are feeling?

Motivating oneself
The mentor helps the executive envision the goals s/he wishes to achieve and plan how to get there. In doing so, the mentor may ask questions such as:

- What drives you to want to achieve this goal?
- What's stopping you?
- What will it feel like when you reach it? (Really good, or flat?)

- What will you want to do next?
- What kind of things motivate you in other circumstances? Can you mix high motivation and low motivation tasks so that you accomplish both?
- How can you use your creative intellect to find silver linings in tasks you would otherwise have no enthusiasm for?
- To what extent is reluctance to pursue something a matter of lack of confidence and how could you gain that confidence?

Recognizing emotions in others

The mentor seeks to make the executive aware of how their behaviour breeds behaviour in others and how to observe the emotional content in other people's speech and behaviours. Questions might include:

- What do you think you might be doing or saying that might make your CEO react to you in this way?
- To what extent and when should you be concerned about how others think and feel about you?
- Do you tend to get the same reaction from people in similar situations?
- Do you think what they were saying reflected what they were really thinking? (For example, was there a difference between their words and their body language?)
- Why do you think they might have felt upset about that?
- How would you have felt in their shoes?

Handling relationships

The mentor helps the executive develop strategies to handle interpersonal exchanges in a way that is more likely to achieve the intended results more consistently. Questions could include:

- How did/do you *want* them to feel?
- How do you manage the conflict between what you think and what you say?
- What is your strategy for motivating others?
- What is your strategy for influencing others more generally?
- What is your strategy for being influenced by others?
- Do you have a wide enough range of responses to react appropriately in most situations? If not, how could you extend your repertoire?

General questions for improving emotional intelligence

- How do you create the reflective space to consider these issues?
- How do you get feedback on the appropriateness of your responses and who from?
- Do you perceive a clear value from investing in developing this aspect of your personal skills?
- Where can you find low-risk opportunities to practise?

While it is not necessary for the in-company mentor, or the mentor in a community programme, to have the competence of a professional counsellor, it can help greatly to recognize when emotional processes are preventing the executive from recognizing and dealing with an issue. Each of the five key domains of emotional intelligence can be observed in what people think and say, and how they behave.

Effective mentors may also look at themselves against this same checklist, or ask for feedback from colleagues.

Clues for the mentor from the executive's behaviour

The following are some of the clues you might look for.

Knowing one's emotions

- The executive avoids talking about how they feel.
- The executive does not admit to behaviour of the same kind as they criticize in others.
- The executive says one thing but does another – and does not recognize that they do so.
- The executive is very defensive to criticism.
- The executive constantly blames other people.
- The executive is not able to explain why s/he feels the way they do.
- The executive seeks intellectual solutions to problems but avoids trying to understand the causes.
- The executive does not recognize repetitive patterns (like always being ill when the work pressure is high).
- The executive consistently gets angry or uncomfortable about addressing certain topics.
- The executive interprets data about his/herself from only one perspective, without accepting the potential validity of other perspectives.
- The executive cannot describe his or her own weaknesses.
- The executive's view of his/her strengths and weaknesses is radically different from other people's.
- The executive shows no apparent interest in how others perceive them.

Managing emotions

- The executive loses his/her temper frequently.
- The executive is often depressed or 'down'.
- The executive exhibits the wrong mood for the situation.
- The executive appears *too* controlled.
- The executive doesn't know when to give up on something that is not going to work.

- The executive finds it hard to delegate, even though they feel they are working too hard.
- The executive is seen by others as volatile, or a 'cold fish'.
- The executive has little apparent sense of humour.
- The executive finds it hard to trust other people.
- The executive has little trust in his/her own intuition.
- The executive over-relies on strengths to the extent that they become weaknesses.

Motivating oneself (not normally a problem with executives, but can occur as an effect of 'burn-out')

- The executive misses goals and targets frequently.
- The executive lacks confidence in their own ability.
- The executive is apt to give up when things get difficult.
- The executive seeks rewards for their efforts unrealistically soon.
- The executive seems to have little drive.
- The executive finds it hard to think of times when they have been on top form ('going with the flow').
- The executive has few strong ambitions.
- The executive is unable to link ambitions with strongly held personal values.

Recognizing emotions in others

- The executive avoids asking others about how they feel.
- The executive interprets data about others from only one perspective, without accepting the potential of other perspectives.
- The executive gives people solutions to problems rather than explores the causes of the problem.
- The executive gets other people's backs up.
- The executive gets into repeated cycles of conflict or poor performance in the team.
- The executive is often baffled by other people's 'unreasonable' behaviour.
- The executive does not see the gap between what other people say and what they do.
- The executive has a poor evaluation of other people's behavioural strengths and weaknesses.
- The executive misses undertones at meetings.
- The executive has low interest in other people's views and perspectives.

Handling relationships

- The executive has little presence at meetings.
- The executive finds it hard to influence/motivate others.
- The executive is often aggressive.

- Other people feel dominated by the executive.
- The executive is not seen as a good team player.
- Behavioural issues seem to be blocking the executive's performance/advancement.
- The executive is not trusted by other people.
- The executive finds it hard to relax in groups with which s/he needs frequent interaction (e.g. people of greater/lesser authority, people with more/less formal qualifications).
- The executive feels his/her efforts are being undermined by others.

These are just a few of many indicators you might observe. Be careful, however, on your own part not to jump to conclusions or make judgements – let the executive reflect on whether and to what extent these symptoms are real or apparent. They will only commit to doing something about them once they have come to a conclusion themselves.

A model of executive mentoring processes

One of the reasons executive mentoring is so difficult to do well is that it operates at several different levels, responding to the mentee's needs. At one

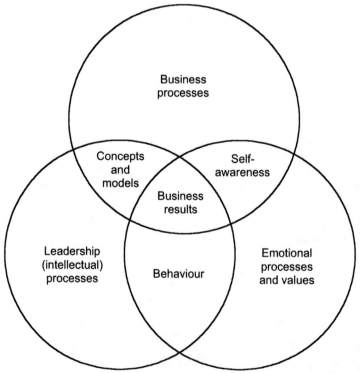

Figure 1.2
A process model

level, it is an intellectual process, providing the executive with challenge. from a source of equal or greater intellect and expertise, introducing greater rigour into the executive's thinking and helping him or her direct the course of future learning, manage personal development and construct viable career plans. The key question here is: 'What and how do you think?'

It is equally about the emotional processes of recognizing personal needs, ambitions and values; about reconciling individual values with the organization and those of colleagues; about internalizing and committing to personal change. The key questions here are: 'What do you feel?' and 'What are your values?'

The emotional and intellectual insights gained through mentoring combine to stimulate progress towards behavioural goals, primarily in the workplace, but also in the executive's private life. 'How do you behave?' is the critical question in linking the executive's intellectual and emotional personae.

Mentoring executives also demands a strong understanding of business context. Breadth here is more important than depth, but the mentor is unlikely to win the executive's respect if s/he doesn't have at least some depth of knowledge and experience, ideally from having done a comparable job elsewhere. The key question here is: 'How do you make things happen?'

To make the business issues real and to provoke rapid insight, the mentor needs to be able to draw on a stock of models, which may be drawn from general management, strategy, behavioural science or other helping roles, such as counselling. The more diverse the mentor's spectrum of models, the more flexible his or her response is likely to be. 'How do you understand what happens in the business?' is central here.

Models tend to operate at the intellectual level although, properly used, they can also open up emotional responses. The business context and the emotional context come together in the creation of self-awareness – insight into personal preferences, styles, needs and drives. In general, the more self-aware the executive becomes – i.e. the more aware they are of how their mind works – the easier s/he will find it to identify and deal with behavioural issues. Self-awareness also helps the executive understand how his or her personal behaviour influences what happens in the business processes for which they have partial or overall responsibility. The critical question here is: 'How do you understand what happens within you?'

When the mentor and the executive work effectively together in all three contexts – intellectual, emotional and business – the potential to improve the executive's personal performance (and, therefore, business results) is high. The fewer contexts they operate in, the less impact the relationship is likely to have on the business. Again, mentors ask a central question: 'How can you contribute more?'

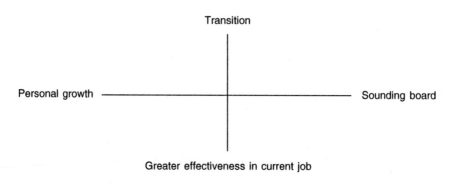

Figure 1.3   Executive mentoring styles

The effective mentor is also able to demonstrate considerable flexibility in terms of responding to variety in relationship purpose. Although in the course of a relationship the executive's need may change dramatically over time, it will tend to be relatively stable in the short to medium term. Where the emphasis is on achieving personal growth through or towards a clear transition in role (e.g. a promotion, or assignment to a project that requires the exercise of new skills), the mentor will encourage the executive to focus on specific competencies and help him or her identify and tackle behavioural barriers that may stand in the way. Where the requirement is for more of a sounding board, to help an executive work towards a transition, the agenda will change from meeting to meeting. Effective executive mentors often begin sessions with a variation of the question: 'So what's keeping you awake at night at the moment?'

What do mentors and mentees discuss?

Figure 1.4 indicates the wide spread of topics that may typically occur in discussions within an executive mentoring relationship. The relationship purpose (and how well it is mutually understood by mentor and mentee) clearly has a major forming influence on what gets talked about. If the relationship is primarily about dealing with issues in the current job, for example, then the discussion will typically involve a lot of reflection on specific incidents and how to learn from past successes and failures. If the focus is on the future, then the analysis will tend to involve a lot more discussion of alternatives and tactics.

In practice, most long-term mentoring relationships move back and forth between these present and future objectives, as circumstances change. Moreover, a dialogue about the future can very easily find itself redirected to current issues, as blockers and enablers in achieving a career goal. Similarly, discussion of what seems like a simple operational issue (e.g. how can I get my team to accept the new remuneration package?) may lead directly to issues of personal development. At the end of most of these chains of dialogue, however, lies some future learning intent – a commitment by the executive to continue thinking around the issue, and/or to taking action, with a view to maintaining the learning process.

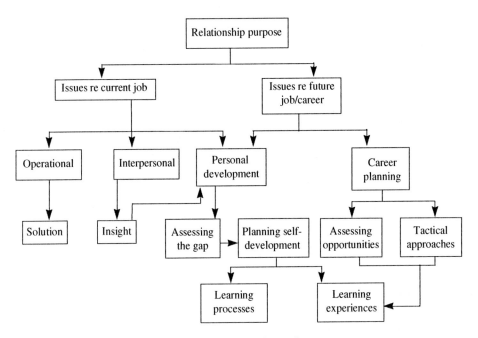

Figure 1.4 What do mentors and mentees discuss?

Among specific topics that occur frequently are:

- coping/stress management
- own and/or colleagues' behaviour and the dynamics between them
- personal fears and doubts
- where am I going?
- recognizing and responding more effectively to repetitive cycles
- reassurance that they are doing the right thing
- drawing on best practice elsewhere
- examining a wider range of options.

Our case studies illustrate this range and more.

What makes an effective executive mentee?

The experiences we have gathered both for this book and in practical work with hundreds of executives suggests that those who get the most value from their experience invariably spend time considering what they want to achieve from the relationship and in preparing for each meeting. They also consider carefully what sort of mentor they require and are open with the mentor about whether they are getting the value that they require from the relationship. Many of them are stung into action about issues they had discussed with the mentor a few weeks before, by the realization that they have another meeting soon. But most of all, effective executive mentees value the opportunity to learn, not just about tasks and skills, nor just about personal, behavioural issues, but about the complex interaction between all of these.

Relationships that work at this level seem to be characterized by:

- very few cancellations or changes of date
- both parties enjoying the experience and being stretched by it
- the executive emerging from each session with a new insight into an issue that has been nagging them, and energized to take action about it
- a high degree of positive challenge, typically laced with at least a modicum of humour.

How to read this book

Part 1 of this book has set out a variety of ways of thinking about executive mentoring and describing this rapidly growing phenomenon. Part 2 moves from the theoretical to the practical experience of both mentors and executive mentees. Part 3 builds on both of these to draw some lessons and common themes from those experiences. Whether you choose to dip into Parts 2 and 3, or to read them straight through, will probably depend on your personal learning style. However, we ask that you will consider, as you do so, how you would feel in these various shoes. How would *you*, as mentor or mentee, have handled this learning situation and what could you have gained from it? We suspect that this is the most powerful way of understanding the essence of mentoring at the most senior levels in organizations.

One final word of caution. In providing analysis of executive and director mentoring, it is not our intention to reduce it to a stark science. Like Keats' rainbow, there is enormous value in retaining some of the mystery in what happens when two people enter reflective space together.

Arguably the worst mentor of all is the person who has attended courses on counselling, NLP, or other analytical styles of helping at a mechanical level, yet has little grasp of the *humanity* that underlies a mentoring relationship. As more and more people offer their services as paid and unpaid mentors, it is vital that executives and directors exercise caution in selecting a personal mentor. Indeed, our advice (and we have deliberately given very little direct advice in this book) to mentees is to decide first about the kind of mentee you wish to be (see immediately above) before thinking about the kind of executive mentor you might wish to engage!

Part 2

Case studies

Introduction

Mentoring of senior executives and directors has remained something of a mystery because of the relative lack of thoughtful and considered accounts of the phenomenon. We have addressed this mystery by seeking such accounts from the parties involved. Nearly all the case studies in this part of the book are in the words of the participants. The authors of this book have written some of the cases, often based on long and detailed knowledge of the people involved. Other writers have contributed the remaining cases, which has enlarged the range of the accounts into countries and sectors where we have relatively little experience.

We do not necessarily agree with all the opinions and approaches described, but we wanted to reflect a diversity of views. We are not making any judgements about what is and is not true mentoring, nor about the quality and compatibility of the mentors. Mentoring is a personal matter, between two 'consenting adults', and the only people who can make a fully informed judgement about it are the participants.

The cases are presented according to sector – private first, then public, then voluntary. Within these sectors they are sequenced by alphabetical order of mentor. To help the reader decide which cases to focus upon we indicate the respondents involved in each and their role.

A Private sector cases

A1 Dinah Bennett, Durham University Business School: mentoring for business creation and development
A2 Liz Borredon, EDHEC, Lille, France: the *accompagnateur*
A3 James Cannon, Director, Right Cavendish
A4 Richard Field, Chairman, Dyson Group
A5 Carl Eric Gestberg, ABB, Sweden
A6 Sir John Harvey Jones, formerly Chief Executive, ICI
A7 Nick Holley, Personnel Director, Lex
A8 Colin Palmer, Chairman, Business Intelligence and his mentee, Nigel Harrison, Managing Director, ACT
A9 Mike Pupius, formerly Director of Business Excellence and Planning, Royal Mail, North East
A10 'Renesse' Group, peer mentoring in the Netherlands (by Lida Beers)
A11 Trude Stolpe, Personnel Director, Axel Johnsson, Sweden
A12 Allen Yurko, Managing Director, Siebe
A13 Kees Zandvliet, HRM Director, Heineken, Netherlands (by Nina Lazeron)

B Public sector cases

B1 Ian Flemming, Dynamiq Consulting and his mentee, Julia Essex, Director of Commisioning, East Herts Health Service
B2 Michael Fowle, Partner, KPMG
B3 Dame Rennie Fritchie, formerly Chair, SW Regional Health Authority
B4 Trish Longden, District Audit (by Judy Weleminsky)
B5 Philip Lewer, Assistant Director, Bradford Social Services
B6 Dan Sequerra, Executive Director, Kirklees Metropolitan Council
B7 David Wilson, Director of Finance of NHS Trust (by Richard Hale and Jonathon Harding)

C Voluntary sector cases

C1 Sir Christopher Ball, Chairman, Campaign for Learning
C2 Dorothy Newton, Acting Director, Federation of Independent Advice Centres (by Judy Weleminsky)

A1 Mentoring for business creation and development by Dinah Bennett and Christina Hartshorn

Dinah Bennett and Christina Hartshorn research and develop mentoring schemes and other processes for executive development in small businesses at Durham University Business School.

In the context of starting and growing your own business, the need for, and practice of, mentoring takes on additional dimensions to the classic mentoring-within-an-organization model.

Creating and growing your own business is not just about learning how to do a new job, and being effective in that role. For owner/managers their 'job' is a way of life. How do business owners think, feel and act? They are very much in isolation with no 'colleagues' at a similar level to themselves to bounce ideas off, or rely on when they are off sick or on holiday. There are no reassurances. With no large organization to support your progress every inch of growth depends on you and your efforts. Particularly critical is the need to form and maintain a network of key individuals or stakeholders. This is not an easy task for anyone starting or growing a business.

An irony which prevails within the Small and Medium Enterprise (SME) community is the perception that individuals are driven to start their own businesses by a strong and overwhelming desire to be independent and in control of their own destiny. Although this is probably true for many aspiring entrepreneurs prior to the launch of a new business, this perception is a myth, as promoters of new ventures discover, all too quickly, that they are required to manage a complex network of external relationships and interdependencies if they are to survive and prosper. Indeed, it has been argued that the competitive advantage of an organization is now a function of its ability to manage this interdependency with stakeholders and that 'the organization is more of a node in a complex network of economic relationships, dependencies and mutual obligations than a production function seeking internal efficiency'.

Thus, it might be argued that the key to success of the small business is the ability to manage and develop this network of interdependencies under conditions of uncertainty and ambiguity. Indeed, the small firm attempts to reduce the risk associated with uncertainty by building personal relationships of trust and confidence with its key stakeholders and 'survival becomes a function of its ability to learn from these stakeholders, educate them, and build trust and interdependency with them'. This network of interdependencies and relationships is also the learning domain for the small firm. Business owners need to articulate and communicate subjective/contextual knowledge (as opposed to objective/largely de-contextualized knowledge, which is remote from the firm's individual circumstances) to appropriate and influential third parties within this mutual learning environment. It must be noted here that the learning in these cases is that of 'self-learning' and not being told what to do. Typical entrepreneurial owner-managers learn by doing, by learning from their mistakes. They perceive being advised or being told what to do as a threat to their autonomy. Hence, mentoring owner managers and those aspiring to run their own businesses brings with it unique problems and opportunities!

The following cases are presented as examples of how mentoring by external stakeholders has helped particular groups of aspiring and existing business owners work through the process of business creation and the different stages of growth.

Women's Business Growth

In the greater Dublin area, a European funded programme assisted about 40 women business owners to consolidate and begin to grow their existing businesses. The initiative used mentoring to complement an action learning-based training programme, and to help the women business owners formulate a formal business plan, necessary if they wished to access funding opportunities.

The mentors were all successful women who owned their own business, many of whom were only 5–10 'business years' ahead of their mentees. They were clearly 'accessible' to the mentees, not just in terms of geography and timing, but also in terms of attitudes and aspirations. They were role models who were not in the stratosphere (in the way that, say, Anita Roddick might be perceived).

The mentors were recruited into a 'mentor bank' and used this group to support each other. Also, when a mentor felt she didn't have sufficient depth of expertise in a particular subject, she would call on the skills of another mentor from the 'bank'. After a careful induction, the mentors were matched on a one-to-one basis with a mentee, and the mentoring relationship began.

As this successful initiative progressed, a set of key issues for mentors was produced by Lucinda Bray, one of the programme co-ordinators, as set out here:

- The mentor's role: midway between mother and devil's advocate.
- The quality of the relationship: open, friendly and informal to increase business and personal confidence.

- Ground rules: where are the boundaries?
- Confidentiality: agreement to respect inside information about each others' business.
- Honesty: to avoid preventable crises.
- Responsibility: to avoid a dependency relationship.
- An 'opt-out' clause: both parties need to be able to request another 'partner'.
- The first meeting: agreeing expectations and ground rules.
- Regular meetings: by mutual agreement.
- Other mentors: using their skills when necessary.

Gleam

Helping recent graduates to create their own employment through starting a business is not a new concept. The Graduate Enterprise Scheme began in England and Scotland during the mid-1980s, and has proven to be a success. However, new graduates are, in the main, just setting off on their career path and almost by definition have few contacts, particularly in the business world.

A recent initiative within Durham University Business School has set out to help graduate business creation be more effective through the close assistance of mentors.

In a large corporate induction scheme, a new graduate would probably have a mentor to show them 'how things are done around here', to immerse them in the organization's culture. Durham University Business School's Graduate Learning about Entrepreneurship, Accelerated through Mentoring (Gleam) scheme has this role with graduate entrepreneurs. The Gleam initiative uses mentors in a similar fashion to introduce the graduate entrepreneurs to the 'small business culture' or local community of practice. By observing how the mentor speaks to potential customers, suppliers and other key stakeholders, the graduate's affective socialization into the role of business owner begins.

But more than that, the Gleam scheme encourages more active participation by the mentor in the graduate's business. Most mentors to date have offered the graduate space and facilities within their own business premises. Often graduates desire to be business owners but are hampered by having no business idea of their own to progress. There is an opportunity in the scheme for the mentor to spin out his or her own ideas to offer to the graduate with the possibility of taking an equity stake in the spin-off business.

Thus the graduate entrepreneur is provided with the physical resources, and access to the 'tools of practice', and can begin the real practice of business as they observe and access their mentor.

The key elements of the Gleam process are:

- A recruitment process: based on making the business community visible and attractive to potential graduate entrepreneurs.
- A protocol of co-operation between mentor and mentee: to cover confidentiality, intellectual property and business ownership.
- Business ideas sharing: so as to transform them into testable market-based business propositions.
- Network sharing: so newcomers know who to meet, and talk to.
- Financial risk sharing: the existing business may wish to share in the new business.

The SME/Banker Linkage project

One potential external stakeholder in every SME's learning network is the bank and/or provider of financial services. Accordingly, every SME and its bankers must nurture the relationship with each other and build an atmosphere of confidence, trust, harmony and mutual understanding if it wishes to maximize the benefits of the relationship and avoid unnecessary stress and potential for conflict. The banks and bankers in particular must move away from 'sitting in judgement' on their SME customers to a position whereby they are integrated fully within a genuine 'learning partnership' which will be of mutual benefit, facilitate risk appraisal and maximize their profitability from the SME sector.

This case study describes a unique linkage project designed to help bankers understand the SME operating environment. It provides a mechanism to raise their levels of empathy and understanding of their role and contribution to the business development process; and to give the SME owner-managers an extra resource to conduct a specific project that they may have had 'on the back burner' for a while. The banker also acts as mentor to the owner-manager, thus ensuring that more SMEs realize their true growth potential and banks can maximize the profitability of their SME customer base. The project highlighted the 'learning interface' between bankers and SMEs and the effectiveness of using short company placements with bankers in the role of a 'hands-on' mentor to identify best practice in respect of this pivotal relationship.

The SME/Banker Linkage project addressed an issue fundamental to continuing and sustainable development of the indigenous business base of an economy. There is considerable empirical evidence to suggest that the owner-managers of independent businesses lack the competence (through lack of appropriate prior experience) to construct growth and development plans which are adequately and appropriately financed. Thus, there is an urgent requirement to assist the owners of growing companies to maximize the existing profitability of their business, ensure that cash is not tied up within the net (current) working assets of their operations and, finally, to assemble flexible funding packages appropriate for controlled and incremental growth. Bankers are well experienced in these areas and, thus, ideally placed to add value to the business development process within their SME customer base. However, there is a parallel need to reorientate bankers in this respect, establish a spirit of co-operation and effective communications between banks and the small business community and establish a mindset whereby the bankers aspire to integrate themselves into the strategic planning process. The linkage project was designed to use genuine business development opportunities as real-time learning experiences for bankers in respect of encouraging this change of attitude and perception of their role.

To achieve this, the project deployed young fast-track bank managers to work full-time alongside the owners of growth companies for a period of six weeks with a view to helping those businesses to maximize profitability and construct growth plans. Prior to these full-time attachments, the participants undertook a short (one week) training programme to prepare them for their secondments. In addition, considerable tutor/mentor and peer group support was available to the bankers and owner-managers during the project period.

The projects were considered successful by all parties to the learning contract – i.e. participating bankers and owner-managers. Success was manifested not only by a feel-good factor for those involved but, also, in terms of commercial (bottom-line) benefit to the participating companies. It was apparent that the bankers had been deployed to support the SMEs in a variety of pragmatic ways. From the SME perspective, the value of the programme was attributable to the provision of an extra expert resource who could accelerate the completion of specific tasks essential to the development of the business.

Each attachment was able to highlight legitimate recommendations for improvements within the SME, which would have gone unnoticed but for the involvement of the bank manager. Often isolated in their decision-making, it was particularly observed by the owner-managers that the bank managers in their role as mentor represented a valuable sounding board – they were both remote from the business and yet sufficiently experienced to provide a valuable alternative perspective.

In broad terms, the SME/Banker Linkage project was a success for all those involved. Specifically, however, success depended on how well the businesses concerned were able to make use of the particular range of skills offered by their secondee. Stage of business development appears to have had a bearing on how successful the owner-managers perceived the project to have been.

However, it is possible to make some generalizations both on the nature of skills demonstrated to be useful during the programme and on the requirements for these skills according to company size. In the main, the value added to the SMEs had its foundation in the following:

- access to business acumen, primarily on business planning, for a dedicated period of time (technical skills)
- the involvement of an impartial professional who could be used as a sounding board on a confidential basis (listening and counselling skills)
- the availability of an extra resource to tackle areas of the business development that may not otherwise have been considered for some period of time (flexibility to respond to the needs of the business).

The Business Bridge project

Business Bridge is the UK adaptation of a concept based on the Plato model from Belgium, for which significant success is claimed. The model has been adapted in a few other European countries, notably in Ireland, which has provided an opportunity for Business Bridge to learn from the experience of others.

In 1995, the DTI provided funds for Business in the Community to run a pilot Business Bridge initiative across three Business Link sites at Hertfordshire, Hereford and Worcester and Leicestershire. The objective set by BITC for Business Bridge was:

> To increase employment and wealth creation by using the experience and expertise of large companies to assist the growth of small and medium sized enterprises.

The concept behind the Business Bridge programme was to create an intimate partnership between large firm managers (group facilitators/mentors) and SME owner-managers, to facilitate a holistic approach to development and growth through knowledge transfer, experience exchange and effective networking.

One of the key challenges is in creating group mentors who can undertake a diverse array of roles, e.g. as facilitator, mediator, communicator, networker, referrer, motivator and role model; and successfully apply a wide range of abilities, i.e. in knowledge transfer, skills development, maintaining a process focus, encouraging co-operation, handling conflict, ensuring relevance and value added, introducing new ideas and thoughts, integrating support and developing strategic thinking and understanding.

The successful implementation of this concept, as proposed by Durham University Business School (DUBS), relies therefore on assessing, developing and embedding four critical faculties within the group mentors. These are:

1 **SME empathy** – before group mentors are able to assist a small business owner-manager, they should be able to demonstrate certain understanding of and empathy towards SMEs.

2 **Value-based learning** – although SME owner-managers may need new management skills it is difficult for them to justify attending formal development programmes if they only learn generic management concepts. Hence group facilitators would need to focus their facilitation/mentoring sessions to value-based learning, i.e. practical, solution/opportunity-based learning that produces results.

3 **Facilitation skills** – multidisciplinary facilitation skills are a prerequisite not only to group cohesiveness but also in maintaining the enthusiasm, participation and interaction of individual owner-managers.

4 **Network interaction** – strong networks help individuals to keep abreast of new developments and knowledge, create new opportunities, enable people to collaborate, share innovative ideas or solve common problems giving greater confidence and credibility to their work.

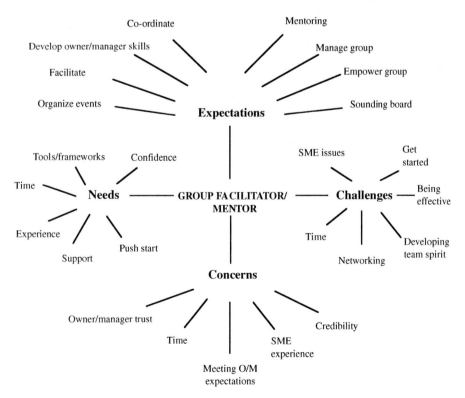

Business Bridge Programme

Figure 2.1 The concept of the Business Bridge programme

A range of issues were expressed by the owner-managers regarding the current challenges they are facing, their expectations of Business Bridge and a number of concerns about Business Bridge mainly relating to the role and selection of the group facilitators. A number suggested some 'best practice' approaches:

Do's	**Don'ts**
act as a catalyst	dominate the group
listen	miss meetings
manage the group	set irrelevant tasks
be prepared	try to be the clever expert
maintain focus	be too formal about setting
convene meetings	and structure
understand personal motivations	
let the SME talk about their	
issues integrate expertise	

Business Bridge aims to maximize the learning at the interface between owner-managers of small firms and corporate managers in large organizations. It is not merely a networking activity, or a business-to-business selling opportunity. The transfer of know-how and experience should be the focus for group interaction, both from the corporate manager to the small firm owner-manager and, vice versa, from the small firm owner-manager to the corporate manager. It is hypothesized that the key practical areas of learning for the owner-manager would be business management systems and skills, generating new opportunities, network development and accessing new resources; for the corporate manager the key learning could be the ability to manage entrepreneurially in uncertain environments with limited resources. This requires understanding what is an effective learning environment, how to create and sustain one and what are appropriate learning processes. This will include focusing on the building of relationships and developing closeness between learners.

Business Bridge is fundamentally about the interface between large and small firms. The rationale for focusing on this interface is that as a learning opportunity there is much that can be learnt on both sides of the interface about and from each other, in addition to the peer group learning that is likely to be already being experienced by many participants. The challenge for all participants is whether the focus on learning can shift from single to double loop learning, i.e. from learning how to 'fix it' to learning why it needs to be fixed and how to learn how to 'fix it'.

As we can see, the use of mentors to help new and existing entrepreneurs to progress is based on the basic principles and tenets of mentoring. These cases have shown how basic mentoring can be augmented to help these entrepreneurs be more effective in business creation and growth. The 'key issues' in these cases are offered as lessons for sharing.

Note

More details about the programmes are available as follows:

Women's Business Growth   Contact Christina Hartshorn at Durham University Business School, Mill Hill Lane, Durham DH1 3LB, tel. 0191 374 7159; or Pat Brand, Contact International Ltd, Equity House, 16–17 Ormond Quay, Dublin 7.

Gleam (Graduate Learning about Entrepreneurship, Accelerated through Mentoring)   Contact David Mullen, Durham University Business School, Mill Hill Lane, Durham DH1 3LB, tel. 0191 374 2223.

Banker Linkage   A programme run in conjunction with NatWest Bank. Contact Dinah Bennett, Durham University Business School, Mill Hill Lane, Durham DH1 3LB, tel. 0191 374 7157, e-mail: dinah.bennett@durham.ac.uk.

Business Bridge   Contact Dinah Bennett, Durham University Business School, Mill Hill Lane, Durham DH1 3LB, tel. 0191 374 7157, e-mail dinah.bennett@durham.ac.uk; or Professor Paul Hannon, Department of Management and Strategy, EDHEC Graduate School of Management, Lille, France.

A2   The *accompagnateur* – a conversation with a French mentor by Liz Borredon

This long story is anonymous for cultural reasons that are explained. We include it in full because it gives a rich account of the development of a mentoring approach in the life of a senior executive. It also illuminates features of French business culture and shows the mentoring style of the interviewer.

Introduction

Shortly after coming to France several years ago, I joined the teaching staff of one of France's leading schools of management. I was eager to explore how mentoring could contribute to the learning process within the existing system. One of the people who generously gave of his time was a French company director who just recently agreed to answer questions concerning his experience of having a mentor as well being a mentor himself.

He is at present managing director of a French company in the food industry, co-founder and director of a group of private consultants, and also co-founder and director of a voluntary association named VCA whose mission is to help unemployed executives find employment. These executives are paired with a mentor who, as far as possible, is either a professional in the same field of business or at least has some connections in that field. VCA does not recruit or advertise in any way. Mentors are attracted through the notion of being of service; some have found work through the VCA and become themselves mentors in turn. They meet between themselves for periods of feedback, review and training. The network's existence is communicated by word of mouth.

The taped interview was in French and thus in places there are explanatory comments that clarify terminology or inference. As little as possible has been cut and the themes covered have not been grouped together under neat headings. The purpose of this structure is to maintain the gradual building of confidence and self disclosure which is similar to the process described in the interview itself; only some of the questions asked are included. Names have been changed to protect privacy.

We had agreed beforehand that we would spend no more than two hours together, during which time he would tell me about two personal situations he had recently experienced.

The experience of having a mentor

Tell me about your mentor.
I had three mentors over a period of five years. The relationship I shall talk about lasted three years. Meetings with my mentor were agreed in advance; they were to be once a month for one year. After the first year, the relationship ended officially. I was told we would both evaluate the year together, and then, if appropriate a new year could be initiated with the same person, or I could ask for another mentor.

What led you to look for such a person?
Conviction; it was suggested and it seemed to be what I wanted for my own personal development. At the time I had choices to make and things to clarify. [*The director is hesitant and vague.*]

   I kept a sort of diary of my experience and how I responded to a given situation. From this writing, I prepared the subjects that I wanted to talk about during the meeting with my mentor. Sometimes I needed to make a decision yet sought clarification from an external point of view, sometimes to check I was right, to verify or confirm that the decision was the right one. You see, one can have the impression at a given moment that things are not working out for this or that reason, then it is good to have someone else's opinion. It could be checking out (verification) of my analysis of the situation, or a decision.

To be sure of your own perception of things?
Yes, that's right.

Verification, what did you expect? Did you want someone to say, 'yes you did well'?
I expect my mentor to be concerned about my personal development. I want him to be concerned about my 'becoming'. From that moment, it is a relationship of trust. This relationship of trust will enable me to say things. I don't necessarily expect him to see things the same way as I do. I don't expect him to take up a position; but to understand me and to ask good questions.

You said you expect him to understand you and ask questions. What skills or competence are you seeking?
Those described by Carl Rogers.

What does that mean?
It means a relationship where the other is not involved in my personal situation, who can stand back from it and is not indifferent to, but concerned by, the choices I make. Caring, not because he is involved but because he hopes for my growth and development.

You do not expect professional competence?
Everything depends on the issues. Certainly in professional mentoring, or professional contact, the mentor will need professional skills. There will be need for specific technical awareness if only to be able to ask the right questions. In that case, yes; otherwise broader relational competence, the competence is to stay external (not judge and not take a position). He must not get involved in decision-making.

You didn't discuss professional matters with your mentor?
Yes I could, but not on technical aspects. Certainly, at a given moment I could have difficulty with my professional life, and need to see clearly what things mean in this context; the mentor needs no technical skill in asking useful questions.

Did this person influence you?
Of course there was an influence – he influenced my stepping back, and seeing things in perspective. Because of my personality, my life style, my profession, I need to take time to stand back and reflect. However, changing mentor over a period of five years was also in order to focus on a given area through the help of a specific person. For example, in the last two years I wanted to focus on more spiritual matters. So it was not the same person with whom it was a question of human relationship.

How did it come about that you started with one, and then changed to another?
I heard about the first person, I met him and then thought that this relationship could be good for me, there would be sufficient trust, and the relationship was relevant to my current situation.

All this is a little abstract, would you allow us to be a little more concrete or shall we leave it at that?
Yes, OK, but what would you like me to talk about?

Well, who was this mentor?
He was a layman within a Christian community to which I belonged, and had a degree of training in the role of mentor.

Do you mean that he was trained to mentor in the field of Christianity?
No, he was trained in what is called the 'helping relationship'. There is a number of approaches in this field; have you heard of PRH (Personalité relations humaines)? Within this structure there is this type of training. A number of people have been trained through this centre.

I was allowed to choose between several individuals that were suggested to me personally. I chose one, intuitively at the start. This was followed by a first meeting – what I call a test meeting – which seemed useful. After this I realized that if I wanted to benefit from future meetings, I needed to prepare for such meetings, that I come to the meeting with a given subject or subjects about which I want to talk, or specific questions that I have, and to progress in this manner.

In our usual everyday life we do not have someone come up to us and suggest several people from which we can choose one to be our mentor. In your case, did you seek out such a relationship?
No; having this one-to-one 'mentor' relationship is characteristic of a number of Christian communities today, and thus it was suggested to me. And it's true, I really didn't know what it meant beforehand. What encouraged me to go ahead was that I suddenly recognized the similarity between what was being offered and other past experience that I had found useful.

And did you know at that time that it was this type of relationship?
No; I suddenly realized that I had a mentor without really being aware of it as such.

To return to the start of your relationship ...
Yes, the relationship was agreed for a period of one year. At the end of that first year, I evaluated the situation and asked to be associated with my mentor for another year. This relationship lasted three years and the reason why it terminated was that suddenly I found myself sharing responsibility with my mentor within the community and thus the neutrality of which I spoke earlier was no longer the same. Not only did we share responsibility but our tasks were mutually interdependent. When I speak of neutrality I mean not involved in my life – for example, my wife could not be my mentor, she is too involved in my life.

Did you end the relationship?
Well, it just became obvious that we could no longer continue in the same relationship.

Were there stages in your relationship with your mentor?
Originally, we were offered a mentor as someone who would help us to integrate the Christian community. After a year, I realized that this was absolutely not the way I had experienced our relationship. That is, when we did the traditional annual evaluation, and he said let's talk about the way we have progressed in your integrating the community, I asked what we were talking about! For me you cannot slice things up. The relationship, the helping relationship with my mentor was not specifically oriented to my life within the community, but to me as a whole entity; everything or anything that concerned me as a developing person. I experienced the focus as being equally oriented on how I dealt with my family, notably my relations with my children, as on professional self-questioning (at that time I had just changed professional role and was

considering what choices I had and wanted to make), and also on my spiritual life. The only rule was, as it were, that we knew the purpose of each meeting.

And who decided that?
I would say that as 'client' in the relationship, I chose the orientation or subject for our meeting.

Earlier you said that you had to prepare for meeting. Who required this preparation, was it your mentor?
Maybe he encouraged me; I was so delighted with the results of preparing that it was obvious to me that this was of great help even after the first two meetings. I found that with my degree of preparation the use of the one hour we were limited to was very efficient. I really didn't want to dilute the time.

So were there actual phases in the relationship that increased effectiveness? Did you get closer? Were there difficulties?
No, there really was not much difficulty. Trust was established very quickly. If there were a stage then it was the first meeting that was really a test. After that first hour, realizing that the relationship could give me something, I dived in. I trusted. I felt secure with this person. I didn't sift through what I could and couldn't say. I trusted the relationship and allowed myself to be guided.

By what?
That's a good question. [*Long pause.*] How can I explain . . . for a start I would say by my intuition. I intuitively felt this would be beneficial, I had no need to withhold, or be cautious. In fact the greater the trust, the more able I was to move forward. That's the first thing; secondly, once I had dived into the realm of trust, I wanted to bring things into light. The image that comes to mind is when you focus light on one aspect, it stands out and you then want to bring everything out into the same degree of clarity.

And was it all your life you were hoping to clarify?
The sense of my life, yes.

Was this your original question or did it come later in your relationship with your mentor?
I had made the choice of entering into a Christian community because the question of meaning had been addressed.

By whom?
By myself. At 40 I had resigned from my professional role precisely because I was not totally satisfied and I was searching for the meaning

of my life. Entering the Christian community was a way of searching for purpose and so when I was offered a mentor, it seemed to be a response to a need I was experiencing. So you see the relationship really was based on trust and I was keen to go as far as I could.

Seeking for purpose is a vast subject: you are married, have a profession, have children, and have interests, conflicts . . .
Actually, most specifically the notion of vocation . . . that is, who I am, and what my place is, what I am here for. So this is what I was looking for in the relationship with my mentor. The work I could do was to review my life, review the choices I had made, things I had done, and it was important to see the significance of these events.

So the point of departure was a certain number of questions. You entered this community because of these questions, you were offered a mentor, you chose one intuitively. Then you say you dived in with your mentor with whom you spent three years and this ended because of certain external circumstances. What progress had you made, or what did you learn?
Firstly there was progress in my relationship with my children. I became more attentive to their lives, I took much more care in communicating with them, finding about their concerns and quite simply devoting more time to family life. I had had difficult relations with them, especially my eldest daughter, and this troubled me; this relationship helped me to deal with this area of my life. Secondly, the whole vocational aspect. For example, an important stage for me was acknowledging that I was very much more of a 'mentor' or guiding companion to someone seeking development than a developer myself. Very practically this meant that I gave up or renounced being sole company director and took on the role of helping senior executives to develop their organizations. You see, the relationship helped me to make very significant choices in my life. I also think that the entire VCA project was facilitated through having had a mentor. It had showed me the foundations on which I wanted to build and it had also given me a certain amount of audacity. I think that one of the very positive consequences of having a mentor at that time, although certainly not the only one, was increasing my self-confidence.

What did your mentor do that helped you change?
Instead of allowing me to fret about not having created anything from scratch, professionally speaking, he helped me to see that I could be effective, efficient and productive in helping others to create; this was much more constructive than dwelling on what I had not done. So I think it is the mentor's role to focus enquiry onto one area rather than another. To help the other see other aspects of reality instead of being identified with one single perspective. Alone, we do not see from many perspectives;

either we don't see, or we don't want to see. The mentor is not there to be kind or accommodating – the mentor can be confronting, or explicit in saying 'you are avoiding the issue' or 'you have overlooked something and it is important to look into it'.

Are there other aspects we need to cover?
Another point is better self-knowledge and awareness of my personal dynamic in terms of potential and development.

By personal dynamic, do you mean energy?
The progress that I experienced did not change the level of energy I had, but it channelled the energy into practical areas where it was needed; my mentor helped me focus this energy. The image I have is of a stream in which there are rocks. The rocks prevent the flow; at certain moments, when the water needs to flow with all its force and energy, but is obstructed, one needs to remove the rocks. I think that in one's life one does not always see the rocks; this is what the mentor does. At the same time he helps confirm your choice of the means you will use to achieve your goal.

Sometimes the mentor made suggestions or advised but only in response to my request. But I always felt free. As I said before, our initial contract was clear: I had choice and I would never have accepted to be limited or constrained by the relationship in any way. For example, at one point I wanted to go on a training programme and my mentor did not prevent me but helped me to take into account factors such as my readiness for the event. The exchange showed me that I should not rush into things and when I finally went, I was really ready, it was the right moment to do so.

Did you help your mentor in any way?
Not during the mentor–learner phase: it was not the purpose. But later we almost changed roles; I was the one who helped him talk through and clarify important life events. I do know that my mentor found our original relationship fulfilling, maybe because we had no problems or obstacles, it was a very smooth relationship. The fact that I had 'dived in', as it were, gave him the taste for work of this sort. From my own experience I know that when someone is really in search for answers, one wants to respond. But we need clarity, trust and wish to progress.

Remember that, every year, the relationship ended because it was only for one year. It could be renewed but this had to be intentional. At the end of the year each of us, separately, evaluated the period. I did this in writing. I was not given a form and this was not imposed but I wanted to reflect on the year and I thought that writing was the best way to do so. So I wrote down what I thought the relationship had given me, whether it met my expectations, and if so, whether this person would be able to help me in what I hoped to achieve, or in the programme I had set myself for the following year. The evaluation aspect is also suggested by the Christian community, just the same way as the mentor relationship was. People respond according to their own convictions. The evaluation is not given to anyone. My mentor did the same thing with each of his mentees over the year, and he considered each request put forward too. Now that the second relationship has come to its year's end, I know that I need to find another mentor; I don't think I should continue with the same person.

So you are looking for another mentor? Do you think it will be someone in the same community?
Not necessarily in the same community. But I cannot envisage being mentor myself to different people in a whole variety of situations without having a mentor myself. I have a number of questions I need to answer. For example, at present I am mentor within the professional field but I have no mentor myself in this context. I know I need to find someone who is able to help me in this field.

Do you think you need a variety of mentors for the different aspects of your life?
I don't know. But right now I think . . . we return to the question of skills or competency, I have the impression I need someone with specific abilities. This is not easy to find in France. There are very few people . . . I know few consultants who offer this type of help. There is one group in Paris which could possibly respond to my need; I need to look into this type of professional mentoring.
   I don't think that the French culture lends itself to this type of work; certainly the Anglo-Saxon culture lends itself much more. If we just examine the type of studies that are on offer. The greatest obstacle in the French system is the 'expert mode'. We are all positioned in terms of expertise, while in the mentoring situation the first requirement or stance is not to know anything. In other words, 'I know that I do not know.' The expert mode is really very heavily ingrained in the French culture. Within our consultants' group we present ourselves as consultants in recruitment of senior executives and *accompagnateurs* of directors and senior executives. I have two reactions from prospective clients: the first one, 'What is an *accompagnateur*?' and the other, 'If you are consultants, in what fields do you give expert advice?'

Explanation of French terminology (1)

In the French language, there is no direct equivalent use of the word mentor. The closest we get to the verb 'to mentor' is the French verb *'accompagner'* which means to accompany or, in the present context, to guide. Sometimes what in English we call 'mentor' is referred to as *'accompagnateur'* which is clumsy; alternatively there is the noun *'parrain'*, which literally means 'godfather'. The same noun 'parrain' is also used for sponsor or for patron. The French noun *'parrainage'* means sponsorship, which is considered as one of the many roles of a mentor in much of the literature. The only French equivalent for mentee is *'filleul'*, which translates as 'godchild'.

More recently, we see *'le coaching'* referred to as a technique used in personal and professional development. *'Le coach'* would be closest to 'the mentor', and *'le coaché'* 'to that of 'mentee'.

The experience of being mentor

You said you are mentor to a number of people. Let's talk about one specific person and refer to other situations if you need to illustrate a point.
I suggest we take the most recent *parrainage*, which I took on within the VCA. The person was called Marc, he was 57 years old and when I first met him he had been unemployed for 8 months.

Within the VCA there is a rule which is that the *parrain* meets their *filleul* once every two weeks, at the *parrain*'s work premises. With Marc, I waived this rule intentionally because he was very destabilized by his current situation. I realized that a period of two weeks was far too long for him to wait. So our contract was that Marc could phone me at any moment he needed to, at his initiative, and if I were not in a position to take his call, I would phone him back as soon as I was able. These calls came to my place of work and sometimes to my home.

I think I need to explain the first meeting, as it was very important, and the point of departure. This man had been an executive in a major textile company from which he was made redundant. He had always worked in large companies, and his field of expertise was export. Being without work, together with its social pressure, had created two situations: the first was that Marc, being 57, was sure he would never find work again. The second was that the loss was experienced as failure and consequently he considered everything else in his life as personal failure. He thought his redundancy, the death of one of his children and the illness of another were part of the same current. All this was explained during the first meeting, and what I needed to do at this point was to identify his unique personal dynamic, and build on it.

The first impression he gave was that of having a force of nature in him – he is a hyperactive person and when he came to see me he was like a lion in a cage. He had quite remarkable energy that was going round in circles and was almost driving him crazy. The lion in a cage is just the right image. We needed to put this energy to work in order to unblock the situation, and the only available work was that of finding employment. And so I was somewhat directive during the first meeting; I refused to accept his claim that he would never find work. Every time he said this, I negated the statement and provided counter-arguments.

I told him, for example, to go and see so and so who was 56, who had found himself in a similar situation; this person had found work and he would explain how he went about it. Thus, from real situations, I could show him that his hypothesis was false as I had proof to the contrary. Here we return to the subject that we discussed earlier: I did not want him to indulge in his feelings, or to collude with him. I was not giving him my opinion, but facts.

There was a sense of urgency during the first meeting. I personally feared he could become very self-destructive, and I had no *parrain* within our association who was available at that time. You see, my role within the association is to conduct a preliminary meeting during which the executive's needs are identified, and we see if the VCA can meet these needs through *parrainage*. If this is the case, I arrange for the new *filleul* and *parrain* to meet.

We both recognized, however, that the meeting was more than an exploratory session. I have explained my perception of the situation but from his standpoint he was obviously engaging himself in what we have previously called a mentoring relationship, as he was under no obligation to explain so much of his personal situation; I had to take on the role of mentor myself.

So he 'dived in'?
Yes, he dived in with complete trust. To Marc it seemed obvious that I would continue the relationship. It was trust that really meant that we were both engaged in the process; above all, trust on his part. I think the fact that I never judged him contributed to his trust. I listened and accepted him except on the topic of not finding employment. The other aspect was that I found him like a man who needed a life-raft at sea; a sort of last resort. We were at the limit of a mentoring relationship of the sort we can offer at the VCA; this was a borderline case as he could so easily have required professional psychological help. I took a risk. I was at the limit of my competence but it is not the first time that I had taken such a risk. I know that the risk of going ahead is greater than the risk of not doing so. The risk of being wrong is almost non-existent as I will not take the person further than I know how. If I know I cannot mentor, I will find the sort of competence that is needed.

You said you would go no further than you knew how to. What do you mean?
Previously you said that a mentor need not know.
Yes it is very ambiguous. What I mean is in terms of understanding the situation. As long as I am able to understand why or how a person reacts, then there is a certain clarity. Once, in another situation at VCA, I decided that I could not continue in the *parrainage* relationship. It seemed that I did not have the keys or means for unlocking a given situation, and no way of helping the person in question. There is an objective, and for the VCA the aim is that the person finds work.

Are you mentor or consultant? Why do you say parrainage?
For several reasons. The first is because our aim is to help the person define their 'professional project' as it were. No one but the person can define personal or professional projects. No one can do this work instead of the person concerned. This is not the work of a consultant. The second, that I have no specific expertise; if I have any it is in listening and staying objective, or not getting involved in another's personal situation. Of course when you have mentored someone over a long period and they tell you they have found work, you are delighted. But it is important to maintain a certain distance in order to help the person conclude what they have to do. The third aspect is to identify just where the person is in their undertaking.

To explain this we would need to get into describing the process of finding work, or the process of personal development or other projects of this nature. I find that there are definite stages in such processes; for example, in finding work there is a first stage of actually defining what one's project is. Another stage is to build one's own network. In order to help someone it is important to know what stage they are at, and to help them position themselves in this process. You cannot travel in another's place, or make transitions for them, but you can tell them where they are at a given time, and this implies identifying the immediate priorities as a result.

It seems that you have a certain degree of expertise in this domain, as you are able to identify the stages in a number of processes – at least you know what they are in advance. You know the terrain or the map and you know how to navigate.
Yes, this is expertise. I do know the terrain that has to be covered, but I will not influence how an individual goes about things; this is their responsibility. I do not influence how long they will take, for example, it is their choice and freedom; the expert would define the stages and the order and timing for going through each of them. However, in the mentor relationship it is a matter of accepting the mentee's feelings about how he will orient himself, even if there is another logic. His way of going

about things is important. We have defined the expertise but in this case it does not include how to go about things.

Do you prepare for your meetings?
It depends on the meeting. I do sometimes prepare and sometimes I don't. Marc's visits were usually unexpected and so I didn't prepare. I gauged where he was at when he arrived. It is possible to imagine that we are far more advanced than a given person actually is on a given day. We sometimes have to go backwards before moving forward. The pacing and attunement to the individual is important for me.

You told me about your joy when your filleul phones to say they have found work. Does the relationship end there?
It depends on the individual mentor, and the relationship of friendship that has built up. Some do stay in contact, others cut the bond, and others do not even let their mentor know they have found work. It is not surprising; I have analysed this situation and concluded that being unemployed is very destabilizing: the moment someone finds work they want to forget the period of unemployment as soon as possible.

So if we return to your relationship with Marc. Are you still in contact with him? Is he still without work?
No, he found a managerial post after four months. He is working in a small company that has just started to export and they needed his expertise to develop that aspect of their firm. He did not want to start exporting from scratch; what he wanted really was to develop a branch that had already been set up.

In what ways did you help him?
To be positive in his search for work. Then, to help him define his project. You see, when he came to see me he said, 'I can do export' and I told him that this was not a project. I encouraged him to explain what export meant, when it took place, how it was developed and with whom, in what type of company and to what country. You see there are many questions that helped him to focus and clarify. He concluded that what interested him was to boost export within a company and not set up an exporting division from scratch. While at the same time, because of his age, to keep an open mind and attention on all openings within the field. There were then a whole series of questions regarding whom I knew, what the best approach was and so on. At this stage, my expertise and contacts were useful.

Were there stages in your relationship?
Yes, the stage that was really important was regaining confidence in himself. I think it vital that any project is developed on the basis of self-confidence.

I was aware of developing this aspect and thus very directive in not allowing him to dwell on not getting work again. I needed to ensure his energy was directed into finding work. The second stage was constructing the project; helping him see what he wanted to do, then encouraging him to define the project that suited him, and to check it out; or help him to check it out.

How did you help him check out his project?
I often explain it in this way: when you hear someone talking of a project you see if the person is talking 'intellectually' or whether the project really matters.

How do you do this? Does he check it out, or do you?
By listening to him. There are two types of verification: the first is operational, namely, the proposed project must correspond to market need. The mentor cannot check out supply and demand in a given area; he could be based in the food industry and the mentee in textiles. We can eliminate this type of validation with the mentor and in any case this is not their responsibility. The mentee needs to seek out someone in their field who is able to testify to the validity of the project in itself.

I am talking about the second type of verification, which concerns the person. The mentor can do this to a degree but we also ask the mentee to talk to people who know him well and are able to see the authenticity and appropriateness of the project for the person, as opposed to something which is faked and unnatural for him. It is clear to see when there is a light in people's eyes when they talk of something about which they feel passionate, when they are really dedicated to something. So this is to seek out how the person feels about their project. This can be their partner, a former collaborator, superior or colleague. Sometimes another mentor from the VCA.

If a project is not considered viable, we must know whether the reason is professional, or personal. At this point the mentor helps his mentee identify the reason. Everything hangs on seeing why the personal and professional aspects do not correspond.

With Marc, this stage was complicated by a number of refusals on the part of companies. Then with the actual company that employed him, there were a number of obstacles to overcome. For example, there was no reply to his initial letter; his immediate response was desperation over another rejection. I had to ask him to consider possible reasons for there being no reply; we had to manage the time of waiting right the way through the various meetings, discussions and interviews. Then we needed to clarify his personal needs in relation to the company's remuneration policy. It was obvious that a company with an annual turnover of 10m FF would not offer the same senior executive salary he had become accustomed to. So having explored what could reasonably be offered under the circumstances, Marc needed to negotiate what was, to him, an acceptable salary.

What, if anything, did this relationship give you?
Firstly the self-satisfaction or joy I have each time a person finds employment. You see, my personal conviction is that we are not made to remain useless or without a contribution to make. Secondly, it confirmed my belief that a man of 56 or 57 can find paid work. Even if I believe this, everyone around me believes the contrary; so this was proof again for me. Now regarding the mentor process itself, I would say what it gave me was encouragement in trusting my intuition regarding the way I should work. With Marc I was far more flexible than we usually are in that I waived the usual rules of procedure. Thus I must trust my intuition in this domain. I had no one else available, I needed to respond urgently – which I did.

Would you have done things differently, on reflection?
Yes, there are some aspects; I responded to certain events in a way that caused us to lose time. For example: when the time came for Marc to type up his CV and the proposed project, he had no machine at home. He therefore used his neighbour's computer and his neighbour had his own personal opinion as to how to seek employment and influenced Marc in changing much of the carefully constructed design. I allowed this to happen. I am not sure I was right not to have intervened.

What would you have preferred to do?
I say this because I had a negative response regarding the presentation of Marc's document. It seemed as if we had gone backwards; the work that Marc had done before meeting his neighbour was far closer to completion than what had been produced. It was a matter of form – the way he had presented his project put it in far less favourable light. I think I should have insisted on the importance of maintaining the original structure earlier.

Did anything surprise you in the relationship or time you spent with Marc?
No, I don't think there was anything that surprised me in this relationship. There were others where I was surprised.

Do you gain something through being surprised?
Yes, it contributes to my work of reflecting on how I do things. I recall one instance when I was not in the role of mentor but more in a support role for the mentor himself. The mentor was helping a young engineer to find work. The person in question was highly qualified; the school from which he had graduated was well known. The mentor was having

difficulty with him and could find no way forward, so I suggested meeting him myself. I was very surprised as I was confronted by someone who was completely blocked and I learnt a lot during the meeting with him; I learnt to refuse to decide for someone else. To explain: we spent one hour together, not discussing his project but a very basic question – namely should he go on holiday or should he not go on holiday and put his search for work first.

This young man's game was to attempt to have me make the decision for him. He would say, for example, 'because you said such and such it means that you think I should stay, and so this is what I must do', and all my work throughout that hour was to refuse to collude and to return the question to him for his own choice. The only contract I had with him was that he decided, and that he then informed me. He left for his holiday. One month later I discovered that his real dilemma was to choose between being a lecturer in a school specializing in the food and agriculture sector and becoming a business executive in this field. You see, I learnt, through what I had done, that sometimes I needed to focus on the process and not the subject. By this I mean, what blocked this young man was not the fact that he did not know whether to teach or go into the food and agriculture industry. The problem was that he did not know how to choose.

Did you help him?
In this meeting I think I helped him through refusing to choose in his place. In fact, he later told me that throughout his life he had always had someone decide for him.

It must have been difficult for him to be told go away and decide for himself.
Well it was not really quite like that. Together we had taken each of the alternatives and he had examined the consequences of each choice. There I had helped him through the questions I had asked. Through our discussion he saw that making a given choice entailed abandoning another possibility; there is a sort of mourning for what is abandoned. In fact he decided there and then at the end of the hour together.

To return to Marc, was there a period of special warmth, or contact?
The warmest moment was when he phoned to say he had his job. That was the strongest moment, but we had always had an easy relationship, although, at the same time, demanding. With the temperament he had, he was not someone who accepted half a response.

And what was the strongest or warmest moment between you and your mentor?
[*Long silence.*] I don't know how to answer that question. There were a few mentors over a long period of time. I don't know how to answer. I think perhaps there were moments of deep confirmation, moments of real personal discovery or of something that made sense for the first time.

Did these moments occur during the meeting with your mentor or after?
During our meeting; it is a little like a jigsaw puzzle when suddenly a piece fits and the whole picture changes. There is a sort of feeling of obviousness that arises within your self. I had very strong experiences of this sort with my mentor in a number of different situations and occasions.

In contrast, you say that with Marc it came at the end of the relationship.
I think that at the moment when someone finds work they come back to life of sorts. They find all their faculties and potential once more.

Is there anything else?
Yes, there is another aspect to all this. In both the mentoring situations I have described, there was an easy relationship of trust immediately. But in another situation trust was developed and established very, very gradually.

I was to be a professional mentor (*accompagnateur*) to a senior partner in a French company embarking on a programme of organizational development. The trust with my 'client' had to be built on what I can only call 'absolute' honesty. This meant that each of us had to be 'up-front' and not to play at hide and seek. I have to explain: my client, and mentee (*filleul*) to be, did not trust me, and suspected that I might personally exploit the relationship. He did not know what motivated me in being a mentor. He wondered why I should want to be of help to him, and we had to overcome that barrier. We did it through my replying to each question that he asked regarding my motives for the relationship. This included explaining why I was devoting time and interest in his specific company, my interest in him as a professional and an individual, and how I felt about the situation. This required a great deal of self-disclosure, and we went backwards sometimes as doubt crept back in. There were times when I doubted we could progress because he was so sceptical and hesitant as to my motives. This was a very significant phase. Then there was a specific moment when he understood the purpose of the relationship and was ready to build on what he had come to trust. He saw the role I could play and the help I could offer to him in developing his company.

Earlier you said that the first meeting is really a test to see whether we can relate as mentor and learner. In this case, the person took a lot of time to test out the relationship.
I was really prepared to let go and lose my client.

Another aspect of the testing stage is the contract: the relationship must be agreed for a given period and a given mission or purpose. This is especially valid in professional mentoring but it is equally important in other situations of personal development or mentoring someone within the VCA structure. I am thinking about another client who asked me to work with him in preparing a specific meeting. We designed the whole event and for this person it seemed obvious that I would facilitate the event with him. This was not our initial contract. I want contracts to be clear.

For you, the mentor relationship has to have a goal and a defined period, knowing that the relationship can be extended or continued intentionally when the initial time limit comes to an end.

Yes, if there is no time limit, or no clear purpose, I fear that we might embark on a sort of discussion when this, surely, is not the objective. So one must be clear as to who the client is. I insist for example on the aspect of authority of the mentor in the relationship with the mentee. You see, once the relationship is established the mentee is really happy to meet with his mentor and then there is a danger that nothing happens. At one moment or another the mentor must say, wait a minute, I am not here for the pleasure of being together, I am here to help you. If I cannot be of further help you must say so, as there are others whom I could be helping. There are many ways of doing this, but the mentor must be the one who takes the relationship back on line with its purpose.

We have come to the end of our agreed time together . . .

Explanation of French terminology (2)

The term 'professional project' (*projet professionnel*) is very common in France; it is rare to talk of career plan because the word career (*carrière*) has connotations when linked to plan or project. It suggests a 'careerist' attitude as opposed to putting together a personal plan for one's professional or working life.

The VCA might seem similar to what Britons or Americans would call career counselling. Part of the mentor's role within VCA could well be to deal with career planning issues, just as the mentor in other situations will use counselling as one of several functions. Career counselling, however, is very rare in France. Some large organizations have what is called '*un gestionnaire de carrière*' (a career manager), but guidance of this sort is not normally found either in business or education.

The noun 'counsellor' translates as '*conseiller*' with the interpretation of 'expertise in a given domain', in order to be able to give advice; the verb 'to counsel' is '*recommender*' or '*conseiller*', which is the same verb as 'to advise'. Sometimes what we would call counselling is referred to as '*écoute active*' (active listening).

There is, however, another dimension – namely that counselling, in terms of 'helping someone to help themselves' with the Rogerian current of empathy and self-disclosure, is somewhat counter-cultural in France. Self-disclosure is considered inappropriate other than in private, personal or medical situations. Credibility is gained through demonstrating cultural sophistication, through reputation and through professional qualification. Authentically expressing feelings can be considered a sign of lack of culture or education. It is therefore often difficult to develop facilitating functions within education or management.

In conclusion, we see how important are the words we use; history and culture are so closely connected to the meaning we attribute to a word that it is difficult to introduce vocabulary that does not correspond to experience.

Postscript

It is exceptional within the French system to have the type of exchange presented in this chapter. The director in question agreed to its anonymous publication in the hope that it contributes to developing understanding of mentoring. I thank him for the time he gave, and for the trust he has placed in us.

A3 The well supervised professional mentor James Cannon, Principal of Cannon Associates, Director of Right Cavendish

This is a thoughtful example of a professional mentor being well supervised. He illustrates how he works by using concrete examples.

I understand by mentoring, a relationship where an individual helps another to reflect on their experience and make sense of it, to explore options for the future and think through the alternatives, to wrestle with a problem in a safe environment where admissions of ignorance, failure or bewilderment are acceptable. There is often confusion with coaching, which is more goal-focused, though using many of the same skills as mentoring and indeed counselling. Counselling is more directed at the person's issues and in non-directive counselling seeks to help the individual to help themselves with their issues towards the outcome that is appropriate for them.

When a group of five of us established Cavendish Partners, a coaching and counselling practice, in 1991, we decided to follow good practice and appoint an external supervisor for our work. The individual, who was known to one of the group, was very experienced and each month would work with us in examining our cases and thinking through how to work more effectively with our clients. At some points these became training sessions, whilst at others they took on the character of individual coaching. Overall the relationship was equivalent to that of a mentor. Working as we did as a group and occasionally on a one-to-one basis, it took a little time to build trust both with the mentor and with each other.

In due course, the agenda broadened from looking at just our clients to a range of counselling issues and approaches as well as from time to time looking at the dynamics of our own team.

The supervisor's style was one of persistent questioning interspersed with advice and suggested approaches. Case studies were sometimes used, but invariably we would work from our own experience. His neutrality and gentle manner ensured that he built credibility and trust with everyone, which ensured the continuation of the process for some five years, only terminating with the sale of the business. His many years as a counselling supervisor ensured that he had much relevant experience when called upon to provide an input as well as the skills of probing and reflecting to help us work with the issues.

Our preparation for each meeting consisted of reviewing our cases of the moment and identifying any which were problematic and needed his input. Certain categories of people, i.e. those who had been with us a long time and were stuck, were automatically brought to the table.

He and I have different academic backgrounds, though both grounded in psychology. It gave us a common frame of reference and facilitated our conversations.

The relationship was limited to work issues and did not stray into each person's personal lives. We described him as our counselling supervisor.

One particularly useful incident came about when I had exhausted everything I could do with a client. The mentor helped me realize that I had done all that was reasonable in the circumstances and another counsellor might bring a fresh perspective. This happened and the client progressed. Without his intervention and the encouragement to let the client go, I might have been tempted to hang on much longer – fearing that to do otherwise might be seen as a failure.

On another occasion, when the team of counsellors began to have internal problems, his unique position – knowing us all well, being seen as involved yet aloof from the day-to-day running – meant that he was able to facilitate a resolution of the conflict.

Following the sale of the business, our supervisor has now joined us as a colleague, though because of his history with us is still useful in providing ideas and acting as a sounding board in a more informal way. Our relationship is one of warm professional regard and I recently have been able to help him as he transitions from an academic background to a more commercial environment.

Myself as a mentor: case study 1 – John

In 1988, the then Managing Director of a small business in the Thames valley sought my help to solve a business crisis surrounding the cost structure of his business. He was a friend and I agreed, out of friendship, with no fee involved. Once this was concluded, he decided he wanted to continue to meet and use me as a sounding board. He subsequently left the business. It was bought by the General Manager, who sought to continue this relationship because of my knowledge of the business and the issues it faced. Initially, the relationship was to provide business consulting advice. As these issues became resolved, the relationship changed towards that of a mentor, that is, someone to provide a listening ear and be a sounding board to enable him to take stock, examine pros and cons, explore hopes and fears and different future options in a safe environment.

We started to meet on a three-monthly basis and by way of preparation he would send me the monthly financial pack along with a note on the key issues of the day. These would range over the whole gamut of business problems. Initially he would pay me per session, but we moved to an annual retainer fee, which allowed for the occasional telephone conversation or ad hoc advice.

The style of the relationship moved along a continuum between at one end a non-directive counselling approach, of active listening and reflective questioning, towards, at the other end, advice-giving and making proposals. My background in coaching and counselling as well as business management provided the skill sets. Occasionally, also, I would facilitate a session with several people to help them evolve a way forward. Whilst my expertise was valued, it was never left in any doubt that he had to make the decisions. He was considerably less experienced in business than me, and my experience provided a major input at times. The greatest value that I sensed was in encouraging him when he felt full of doubt, by helping to look clearly at an issue without deviation and keeping focused on the critical issues of the day.

A major issue was developing an information system that accurately measured what was going on. My role here was to ensure that the issue was not allowed to die until an adequate solution was implemented.

The relationship continued for about three years until he felt that he wanted a fresh input and sought advice from someone else. After about two years, we met again for lunch and he reflected how helpful my input had been: in particular in keeping focused on the key issues, facing up to some of the tougher decisions, thinking through more complex issues, especially about people and brainstorming ideas about getting business.

In retrospect, I learnt about the power of building a process over time, one that is often denied with a short-term consulting intervention. However, I was sometimes fearful that I was not really adding value. The opportunity to follow through and evaluate with the client the strategies meant that we had before us a living laboratory from which we both learned.

Myself as a mentor: case study 2 – Peter

Peter is a brilliant scientist, but lacked a range of interpersonal skills that were becoming increasingly necessary as he progressed in the company and acquired staff and Board responsibilities.

Our relationship started as a result of an introduction from a mutual acquaintance and we began our work by looking at a range of difficult (for him) situations and working through some alternative approaches. When we met the next time we would examine what worked and what did not and how he might do things differently. When the time came for major reshuffling of duties, we examined the issue in some detail and I helped him develop a plan. Up to this point the relationship might best be described as a coaching one.

From then on, the substance of the meetings changed from specific issues to ones of a more general reflective nature on his work, the problems he faced and his relations with his boss. The role became then one of mentor, rather than coach, and consisted of much listening, reflective questioning and very occasional sharing of some experience.

However, his boss, who was sanctioning the fee, believed there were still unresolved issues and we therefore had to return together as a threesome and explore and clarify the issues before re-contracting on our own work and pursuing our coaching again.

Thoughts about mentoring in general

At the heart of counselling, coaching and mentoring is the 'Aha' factor: that ability to create in another an insight that causes them to view the world in a different way. The pressures of modern organizational life are only managed by attention to detail and extreme focus on the issues of the moment. The consequence of this response is increasing tunnel vision. Yet many of today's problems require increasingly creative solutions. Supporting another through a helping relationship that allows that person to think more broadly – outside the box – is therefore of growing importance.

The question that all managers and directors need therefore to answer is, 'Where is your source of challenge and insight?' Whether this is provided through a formal mentoring scheme or by someone on a more informal basis, it is becoming a necessity for all.

A4   Richard D. Field, OBE: a company chairman and a principled mentor

Richard Field is Chairman of Field Enterprises Ltd and Chairman of J & J Dyson plc. He was the 1996/7 Master of the Company of Cutlers in Hallamshire – the body that represents cutlery, steel and associated industries in South Yorkshire. He was the first Chairman of the Sheffield Training and Enterprise Council.

My belief is that mentoring is not about trying to change others – this creates a quick fix, which does not last. A fundamental truth is that if you continuously improve yourself, then people will come to you. If I am a role model, and I exude love, then I am able to respond to what they need. It is about preparation more than planning. Planning is working backwards from a goal; preparation is like strategy in a business – following the 'plan, do, study, act' cycle. When he was having terrible difficulty setting himself a one-year plan, I asked a friend who was his role model. He said, 'Jesus Christ'. Did Christ plan? No, he prepared.

A mentor is a friend, a coach, a judge and an encourager. You have got to have enormous trust and a long-term relationship – which can be created in moments. To do this you have to be prepared to be totally vulnerable – when I have given trust, I don't think I have ever been let down.

The first mentor I can recall having in business was Jim Binnie, the HR Director of Bridon Wire. I had just been promoted to Chief Accountant at the age of 28 and given responsibility for 60 people (including group administration and computers). I had no formal management training, but Jim took me through a Harvard MBA by giving me Harvard Business Review articles and talking them through with me. We became great friends. When I set up my industry's Training Board and was the first Chair, he had already retired, but he came back to work to become the Chief Executive. I learned from him that everyone has something that adds to one's own knowledge.

Another mentor was Sir Brian Nicholson, when he chaired the Industrial Society and I chaired their Executive Committee. I wanted to be the very best Chairman I could be, and he was the best I knew.

Michael Woodhouse was another who took me under his wing. I think he was Deputy Chairman of Courtaulds and I met him when he became Chair of the Prince of Wales Volunteers. He gave me leads to see the best practice of leadership in action in the USA.

The mentor who I have learned the most from in business is my Chief Executive at Dysons, Mike O'Brien. I used to say that this or that isolated task needed doing, but he showed me how we needed to move the whole organization forward together. We are there to plant trees that we may never see fully grown. I have learned more from him in terms of business than from anyone else, and I owe him a great deal.

Now, on the business side, as I change my role to business consultant and facilitator – focusing on enhancing others full-time in many organizations – I spend time reading and learning from others, watching and listening to others, and listening to myself. I noticed that I had lots of will to drive forward projects, but a yawning gap, an emptiness in my spiritual element, which I have begun to fill by thinking things through and listening. In organizations I believe that *values* are central, and for individuals I believe it is about living by certain *absolutes*. For me these absolutes are: absolute honesty, absolute purity, absolute selflessness and absolute love. You have to exude these. But mentoring is not about categorizing things, it is about being the best you can be, and especially about always respecting others – not intruding in their path.

I have a number of spiritual mentors. The Provost of Sheffield Cathedral and I meet for breakfast every six weeks or so after a service. He gives me responses to my questions about Christianity. As Master Cutler, my Chaplain for the year was Canon Mike West, who is a great friend. We met once a month for the year before I became Master Cutler to discuss my bible reading. Then, at the start of my year, he led a quiet day, in the manner of Quakers, for myself and twelve people who have supported me during the year. John and Ann Carlisle are also mentors, not only in business, as we also share insights into Christianity and Rudolf Steiner on Saturday afternoons in a group which meets weekly.

I do Tai Chi every day. My Tai Chi master is called Reza Hezavah, who has taught me one morning a week for the last seven years. He teaches not only Tai Chi but also a philosophy of life. Before my 8.00 am Saturday morning run with the Sheffield running group, I meet and learn more about eastern philosophy with Paul Thompson. The running group is also important as a support group exploring mind, body and spirit; loving learning and loving me for who I am.

I gain insight from the astonishing wisdom of the world from my morning walks on the moor beyond my house; also, by giving myself fifteen minutes of quiet time, so that the still small voice within me, which must be the final arbiter, can be heard.

My physical mentors are Reza with Tai Chi and, for ten years until 1991, Joe Mappin with Jujitsu. Some time after I had completed my black belt, I asked Joe if I could proceed with my second Dan, the next stage in the sequence. He said that he would let me when he thought I was ready, when I was disciplined enough. I said that I attended twice a week for training and practised most days – didn't that show commitment? He then said that if I attended the gym every morning at 6.00 am seven days a week (which meant getting up at 5.00 am) then, when I had shown this commitment for long enough, he would let me start to train for the second Dan. After 17 weeks of this routine, he said he would take me on. Fifty-two weeks later I successfully took my second Dan. You realize at 5.00 am on a freezing dark morning that there are no boundaries; these are all in the mind. Life is wonderful – awesome.

My PA, Jenny Parkin, is also a mentor, giving me feedback on my meetings and speeches and how they might be improved. My wife, Pippa, keeps my feet on the ground – she helps me to see the downside of projects and to focus my mind to persuade her of the upside. I have also received mentoring support from my younger and elder brothers and my mother and father. All three of their sons have achieved what we are through them.

I currently mentor 11 people, and four of these pay me for this. I have used the fees to support community projects. I ask them to send me a fax each week saying how they are going with the issues that they raised the previous week and anything else that concerns them. I fax back to them each Sunday, sending a common message from my learning during the week, and also a message unique to each of them. I encourage them to look holistically at their life and to see if it is in balance; to see what they need and if I can support them in that.

If they commit to something and then do not follow it up, I remind them that they have not done what they said they would do. Sometimes I say, 'I didn't know that "not too bad" was in your vocabulary.' My greatest contribution is to allow them to realize their potential – this is so liberating.

I see them face to face as well, of course. I meet one person for breakfast once a month. Another (who is Group Chairman of a hotel chain) I spend half a day with. We go for a run together and play chess, and then we have the mentoring. This has developed so that now I spend time with her leadership group of the company in the morning and then we have the one-to-one session in the afternoon.

One is a hotel manager in Hong Kong, so I only see him when I am on business there or when he is in the UK.

The people I mentor are varied: a PhD student at Cambridge, a linguist, someone who is unemployed, as well as business owners, managing directors and senior executives – both male and female. I must be totally dependable for them; I am always there. I do not miss a weekly fax unless I am away – in which case I let them know in advance.

I do not go looking for people to mentor – they find me. Enlightened leaders are like the calm within the storm, and people move towards them. Nor do I have any timescale for the mentoring – it is like family:

I am part of their path for however long it takes. If they do not fax to me they still get my fax, and sometimes they say that during the difficult times that was what kept them going.

I believe in the simple path of Mother Theresa – where the fruit of silence is prayer, the fruit of prayer is faith, the fruit of faith is love, the fruit of love is service and the fruit of service is peace. I also believe that the fruit of peace is silence.

A5   Carl Eric Gestberg, ABB, Sweden – thorough processes support an internal scheme

This corporate case study, based on a presentation at a mentoring conference in Stockholm in 1998, shows how strong support from the CEO of a major corporation, combined with thorough processes of support and development, can lead to a successful executive mentoring scheme using internal mentors.

For ABB, mentoring is a continuous process. In 1991, we had 150 women involved in mentoring relationships; in 1992 there were 250. In 1998, we had 3000 people involved – both men and women.

We have integrated mentoring into competence development. There is a natural cycle for knowledge recirculation, and mentoring is part of this. Mentoring is also a cycle of planning, meeting, documenting, reviewing, doing. If you go on a management training course, mentoring is one way of distributing new knowledge.

The mentee has to be:

- curious
- clear what they want out of the relationship.

We provided self-assessment materials to help them with this.

Mentees often start with the misconception that they cannot contribute to the mentor. We encourage them to think of it in a different way, as a senior mentor and a junior mentor.

We put all the responsibility on the mentee to find the help they need. Once you have established your criteria for a mentor, you go out and find them. You use or create your own network, who can help direct you to the right person. HR's role is to stay in the background and offer advice when it is needed.

ABB Sweden has 130 companies, so they could easily find a mentor outside their own company. They could also go outside ABB, if they wanted, but that is very rare.

The mentoring programme received a considerable amount of support:

- The CEO set an example by becoming a mentor himself.
- We set up a steering group for the mentoring programme, as a customer group of HR.
- We set up a series of review and support meetings, amounting to about 8 hours across the year.

- We developed a network to aid recruiting of mentors.
- Mentors and mentees meet once or twice a year with the CEO to review the programme.

The marketing process is:

- an introductory half-day
- a launch seminar
- mentoring meetings
- review and relaunch.

Mentoring is a rolling programme. People who come off the programme after 12 months often act as role models for new starts. People typically take two months to find a mentor and have a training session within 2.5 months: the sessions cover issues such as communication, formulating goals and what to do if it goes wrong. Their companies pay for it.

Mentors and mentees typically meet 10–12 times a year. They also attend a series of six meetings with interested people who share ideas about wider management topics.

A6   Sir John Harvey-Jones: the self-made top executive passionate to help others

Sir John was Chief Executive of ICI and, since his retirement, has written, broadcast and advised about company direction. He is well known in Britain for his book and TV series 'Trouble-shooter'.

I had one boss, who looked out for me as a mentor and general developer, but he did not have the skills to do it properly. I remember his waffly interventions with affection. Apart from him, however, I did not have a mentor and I regret it.

I am a strong believer in taking stock of oneself every year: where you've come from, where you want to get to. Unless you look back, you are not aware of having gone anywhere. The problem is, it is very hard to be honest with yourself, so you need someone else to review things with you. Since so few senior jobs are described with any clarity, it is even more difficult at the top to know if what you are doing is any use or not. It is demotivating to operate in a vacuum.

As a mentor myself within ICI, I saw the task primarily as an on-line activity. I spent about 15 per cent of my time on it. I offered advice to subordinates rather than peers. But the biggest value is having a mentor off-line, not least because there is less chance of cloning. An off-line mentor also often finds it easier to be sharp and direct. People can usually do a lot themselves about areas where they are not performing well, but if it comes down the line it can be seen as biased. The off-line mentor, on the other hand, is an independent source and therefore more credible.

Good mentoring involves a lot of common ground, an element of trust, and a belief that your advice is disinterested. Building trust is very difficult – you have to spend a lot of time to make it happen.

Justifying the investment of time is not difficult. I have always believed that developing others is the key to everything in management. I am not a believer in doing other people's jobs and I am not a supervisory style of manager.

Because I was not operating as a formal manager, I found that there was almost always a period of anger and rejection by people I was helping. There was a fear and a lack of belief that it was being done in a constructive way. Then there was a tendency to swing to the other extreme – over-dependency. So I had to work to make sure the people I was helping owned the problem.

I coped by always offering a range of choices. I never gave a single blueprint. I would tell them that they didn't even have to make use of any of the ideas I would present; that they were quite capable of generating a few more. There is no single solution that works in management – only the one that you own. But I was still thrilled when they took my ideas up!

Essentially, what I've been doing in 'Trouble-shooter' is mentoring. I get people to look at things differently and form their own action plans. It helps that I sometimes see things they don't.

The payback for me is satisfaction at seeing people grow. There is no greater delight, apart from creating something yourself. I take inordinate pride in the people I have discovered.

Everybody does need a mentor, probably more so the further down the organization you are. At the top, the problem is getting people there: many people have the capability but not the assertiveness to push themselves forward. The mentor's role is often to help them gain self-belief, continuously to raise their horizons; helping them set achievable objectives and gradually ratchet up their self-belief until they are doing more than they ever thought they could.

I also found that mentoring helps to keep the mentor's feet on the ground. There is no question that, if you retain a close relationship with someone younger, you develop sensitivity to what is happening in the organization. I found I used them as a sounding board and they gave me a clear perception of how I appeared to people down the line. It gets more important to do this as you get older.

Right back from my naval days, I helped several people through to admirals or captains. I built a bond with them that lasts a long time.

What should you look for in a mentor? Trust is critical. You are not trying to produce cannon fodder for your own outfit. The responsibility is to the individual.

The mentor also has to be someone you admire – self-selection is important. If you are lucky enough to get advice from someone you respect, you are half-way to achieving your goal.

Very few organizations acknowledge or reward successful mentors and coaches – people who may have brilliant records of finding and developing talent. There is no parallel line of development to become, say, mentor-in-chief. When we discussed promotions and appointments at ICI, I would always discuss a person's ability to develop others. We had numerous people who did not go further in management themselves, yet who were absolutely superb in developing the right attitudes and aspirations in younger people. But we didn't reward them by any other means. They got paid for past performance, not for developing the future talent of the organization. Now, I would pay a mentor's allowance or find some other way of giving greater recognition to the importance of what they contribute.

A7   Creating a mentoring culture in Lex by Nick Holley, Personnel Director, Lex

A corporate case study of an HR initiated, but business driven, mentoring culture: low on bureaucracy and control; high on relevance, measurement and top-level support. Nick Holley now works for Prudential.

Why have we introduced mentoring in Lex?

At a European Foundation for Management Development conference in 1994 Paul Evans of INSEAD issued a challenge:

> The world is full of solutions looking for problems.

It certainly challenged our thinking about management development and has been at the front of my mind ever since. It has been central to Lex's approach to mentoring. We didn't start by saying, 'Mentoring is a good idea, how can we use it?' We started with a number of issues where more traditional approaches did not work or did not fit our culture. We saw that mentoring could be an answer, tried it and then ran with it where it worked.

Our learning point has been that we do not have a Lex mentoring programme, we have a number of different issues where mentoring is one of the solutions we are using.

How have we used mentoring in Lex?

Let me start by briefly outlining some of these challenges and showing how we applied mentoring. But beware! This is what we did and what worked for us. That does not mean the same approach will work for you.

Management retention

Management development is about ensuring we have the right skills, attitudes and experience in our management population to meet our current and future business needs. It is as much about recruiting people with these skills and retaining them in the business as trying to develop skills which people do not have and maybe never will have.

In our succession processes we have identified a number of people at executive level that we feel are critical to our future. In each case we have allocated to them a member of the executive team (including the Chairman and Chief Executive) as a mentor. In each case there is no direct reporting relationship. Geographically there needs to be some likelihood of them getting together, and the mentors tend to have strengths where the mentees have developmental needs.

The mentor is tasked with ensuring the mentee has:

- a clear view of the value we place in them
- a job that is stretching
- a development plan which is actively supported
- an ongoing dialogue about their career which takes into account both the company's and their needs
- appropriate reward and recognition
- access to the Chief Executive.

The executive team then reviews this checklist and the performance of the mentor.

The programme has been a huge success. How do we know? Whilst turnover in the general management population has remained steady, in this population it has halved. It is clear that one cannot make a causal link, but there is strong circumstantial evidence. To back this up we also talk to the people involved to understand what impact the programme has had.

Some of these questions are quantitative:

- How many times have you met? (on average 4/5 times a year)
- Do you intend continuing with the relationship? (yes, 13 out of 15)

These are busy senior executives. If the process was not adding value they wouldn't continue with it.

Some of these questions are qualitative:

- What have you got out of it?
  Career Guide: Guidance, help and wise counsel in managing careers:

  I can get some advice from someone who's been through it before.

  Consultant: Support in making difficult decisions/addressing specific issues, brings the bigger picture or another viewpoint:

  It has given me a totally different view of my role. It has helped me become less tasky so I can delegate and empower more effectively.

  Coach: Fill in specific skill gaps:

  His skills are in areas I need to brush up on.

Counsellor: Help with personal issues – stress, pressure, time management, managing upwards:

> He helped me through a particularly bad patch with my boss.
> He gave me good advice on what to do.

One person put it very succinctly:

> The most valuable piece of management development I've ever had.

So valuable that we have now extended it to the next layer of management with people who have been mentees now becoming mentors.

Middle management development centres

For the next layer of management we run internal development centres. These are designed to give self-insight through 360° feedback, psychometrics and exercises over a three-day residential programme. They help people think not about their current role, but about their next career move. The problem has always been lack of follow-up. Their boss is usually more concerned with their current performance than their longer-term potential, if it might mean losing the best people

To overcome this, each participant has a mentor who, as well as fulfilling the role of sponsor/coach etc., is tasked with ensuring that the individual follows up on their commitments and that the organization provides the requisite support.

Training delivery

Most of our managers are pragmatic learners. They are not interested in the theory but about how to apply it in practice. Thus we support a number of training programmes with ongoing mentoring. In the case of sales training this will involve mentoring around a specific sales pitch as well as classroom learning.

We have also used it as a measure of the success of the programme. The mentoring is offered but is not compulsory. People are not stupid – if they value mentoring and it is improving their performance they will avail themselves of the opportunity. Thus we have tied the fees charged by external training suppliers to the amount of pick-up of the mentoring.

Ad hoc support

Our senior managers have personal development plans. The challenge is making sure they are relevant. If they are relevant, the managers are more likely to follow them through. If they are relevant, the learning is more likely to result in performance improvement.

We have helped the managers to establish mentoring relationships. These have sometimes been informal relationships with senior managers in other non-competitive organizations:

- An MD with a marketing background who is increasingly getting involved in operational delivery. We have built a relationship for him with a senior retailer from one of the UK's top grocery chains. He is strong on delivery and measurement, but needs help with his marketing. The two meet regularly to exchange experiences and tips.

On other occasions, they have been formal relationships with professional external mentors:

- An MD who sees his ability to help his people learn as critical to meeting the challenge of increasing customer demands and competition. We have established a mentoring relationship with one of the UK's leading thinkers on management learning. The MD has got so much value that this person now works with other members of his senior team.

The key in both cases is that we have acted as a matchmaker but it is up to the two people to make the relationship work.

As a result of our beginning the process and the successes that have happened, mentoring relationships are springing up all over Lex. In many cases, we have no idea that it is happening. Shock horror – we aren't in control! Perhaps that is the reason for success.

Why has mentoring been a success?

- **Pull v push**
  Success has not come from a big central push. We have provided the initial idea but people have adopted it, seen value in it and run with it. Ownership in the business, not at the centre, is everything.
- **Networking**
  Our role has been to spread the word that it is a valuable tool to prompt people to look at it and to provide a framework. Credibility has built over time, based on a lot of face-to-face communication.
- **Non-bureaucratic**
  Paperwork may have a role in some organizations but not in ours. Paperwork would kill it, so there isn't any. Indeed, if need drives it and ownership is everything, why do you need paperwork?
- **Training**
  One thing we have driven is high quality training. Every management team has been through a half-day of training led by their Group MD. This has been highly interactive, role-play based and light on theory, driven out of

each person's specific needs. This has been linked to the importance of coaching and much of the session has focused on practising coaching as a skill.

- **Measurement**
  Credibility has grown because we have been active in measuring its impact. This has led to the spreading of best practice and is part of the ongoing communication – by this we mean communication based on successes in Lex, not on irrelevant or academic case studies.

- **Leadership**
  It has been critical to have active involvement from the top. Our Chief Executive has stated that management development is one of his three key drivers and a strategic core competence for Lex. The top team value mentoring as a core part of this commitment. He and all the Management Board have been actively involved as mentors. They were the first people to use the process. They have seen the benefits for themselves, giving credibility to the idea and providing role models.

- **Culture**
  Mentoring fits our culture:
    - It is not time-intensive.
    - It is cost-effective.
    - It gives practical advice that people can apply.
    - People learn from people who have 'made it' rather than academics or consultants who haven't worked in our business.
    - Mentors already have respect so they are listened to.

Conclusion

What we have done is not what you should do. But I think there is a clear message here: be absolutely clear why you are doing it – what is the issue mentoring is addressing?

If the answer is, 'I read a good book about mentoring and I'm looking at introducing it into my organization', then be careful. The issue for you might actually be very different from the issue for us.

A8 Colin Palmer mentors Nigel Harrison: two accounts of an experienced director mentoring small business leaders

A8a Colin Palmer, Chairman of Business Intelligence and of the IMPACT programme mentors Nigel Harrison, Managing Director, ACT

Colin Palmer is Chairman of Business Intelligence and a Visiting Lecturer at Imperial College School of Management. He has been Personnel and IT Director, then Deputy Chairman of Thompson Travel, and IT Director of Unipart. He operates as a mentor of small businesses directors, including the Directors of ACT, helping them to grow their business while maintaining balance in their lives.

I became a formal mentor as a result of finding myself doing it informally, and people telling me it was helpful. I enjoy helping small businesses, and this leads to my biggest fear about the work – wondering whether it is valuable. It is so pleasant sitting there, chatting. Yet when I check, they always say they get value from it. I also have some concerns about how far you can go with relationship issues. I often work with two directors in a business, and I find that one party tends to be happier with their business relationships than the other. One normally has greater clarity about what they want in life, and they go about getting it. The other takes responsibility for what is left to do in the business, and suffers for it – they catch the balls that the other one drops. I am thinking about a case other than ACT now, where one individual enjoys the bright ideas, the opportunities, the networking, and neglects the commercial aspects. The other takes a monitor–evaluator role whenever they are in discussion, and neglects their own creativity. This leads to stress.

I have a process for my work. I start asking about personal interests and commitments, and personal goals and vision. Then I relate this to the business. One of the most useful things up front is to clarify why they are doing this – what their interests and motivations are, and how the business fits into their lives; where they want to be in five or ten years time, and what this means in business terms. It becomes a self-fulfilling prophecy if they keep it in mind. It is also useful to look at where things go out of alignment – especially when working with two people.

I help by reflecting back what they say, by being a role model (having built up a business myself), and by asking good questions – asking the questions behind the questions. So, if two directors of a business say to me that they want to achieve a particular figure for profit next year, I might ask 'Why?' five times, to get back to the fundamental issue. I also end up giving advice on issues of 'protection' and 'exit'. Because I have been there, I talk them through such issues as professional indemnity exposure, registering trade names, preparing for due diligence searches, which require specific advice.

I prepare for meetings by ringing them a few days before and having a chat about what is on their minds. On my way to the meeting I will go back over the notes of the previous meeting to refresh my memory. They seem to value the fact that I am older and ostensibly wiser. This helps in that I can foresee things that will turn up; it is a hindrance if I assume things – then I can keep probing for something and it is not there.

The relationship with Tim and Nigel has kept going for two years because it has been very flexible. At the beginning of this year they had a rough ride. I backed off, and I didn't charge for two sessions: they can pay when they can afford to – I will take the pain with them. At our latest meeting we discussed where I could add more value and where they are missing help. So I am going to sit in on their next, regular shareholders' meeting. I will see if they need help in monitoring the business and whether they need to consider new structures.

One problem with this work is that small businesses are much more volatile than larger ones. This is a challenge for the role of the mentor. Can I be expected to raise sufficient questions to alert them to all the issues? There are limits to my role. It is about the people and their development of the business, in relation to their personal needs. I am not there as a non-executive director focusing on the business. I offer them personal support in the context of their business.

The stages of the mentoring relationship that I think about are the ones described in the first chapter of *Mentoring in Action* (Megginson and Clutterbuck, 1995, pp. 30ff.): establishing rapport, direction setting, progress making and moving on.

Benefits for the mentor? Absolutely! What I learned with Business Intelligence I have been able to apply at ACT.

My warmest feelings come when people tell me they've got something out of it. My biggest regrets are not spotting some of the things I should have explored earlier, or not being challenging enough.

Mentoring relationships can evolve – there is one public sector IT Director who I used to mentor, and he still rings me up to check out big decisions. He rang me recently to 'seek my permission' to look for another job. I met with him and helped him sort through the options, but I did not help him enough to face up to the issues in his current work.

With people who I am currently mentoring, I also help them in networking when they ring me and say, 'Do you know anyone who . . .?'

I think that mentors are most useful for directors at points of crossover and change, when the business has reached a certain size and they don't know what to do next. In considering taking on a mentor at this level, chemistry is hugely important – can you get on with them? That and their credibility. Have they had relevant experience, and can they ask good and challenging questions?

I can't think I have ever had a mentor. There were one or two bosses who I related to well, and still meet up with even today. I think my lack of mentors is a reflection on me – I have an unreasonable view of my own self-reliance and self-sufficiency – I have a sense that there is a weakness in confessing the need. This is pretty stupid really!

A8b Nigel Harrison, Managing Director, ACT, interviewed by Melanie Sinnett

Nigel Harrison is a successful author and Managing Director of a growing consultancy business. He is mentored by Colin Palmer and candidly discusses some previous, less successful mentoring relationships.

When I talk about the part that mentoring has played in my career, it is easiest to work backwards, because the most straightforward contract is the present one with Colin Palmer.

It was very rational, because we asked David Megginson to find us someone, after years of searching. We wanted someone to help us to move the business forward from turnover of three-quarters of a million to about five million, and someone who would fit in with our culture. And Colin fits the bill. He has done that with the same sort of business that we are in, and what we also like is that he has a definite process: as we are process consultants, he does the same thing to us that we do to other people. He helps us focus on priority issues. So it is a reflective device for us. He has the credibility and experience and he is just a little bit older than us. He has seen the next step – the one we want to take, Tim (my co-director) and I. So he is helping us to develop ourselves: think ourselves into the psychology of running a medium-sized business rather than a small one. We have never believed we were a small business – we've always believed that we are a big business that just hasn't got big yet! The way that Colin thinks helps us, and the way that he has had contacts helps us. So that's very rational and straightforward – and it works very well.

One of the major things he's helped us, the two Directors, focus on is our personal interests. We are very strong strategic managers for the business – we have been established for about 10 years now – but he has helped us focus on where we were as individuals. And he helps us to think, funnily enough, like a small businessman about things like what we should pay ourselves, what sort of pension we have. We have got used to putting ourselves last. As the business has grown, we have cut our salaries when we've been struggling and he has helped us to realize that although we do take the financial risk of the business, we do need to make adequate provision for our pensions, for example.

He has looked at our strategy, too. Our strategy depends on growth, so he has helped us to look at the key things that are holding us back from achieving this growth strategy, the personnel that we need to get there and those sort of things.

Let us contrast this experience with our earlier attempts to find a mentor.

The first person we tried was from Manchester Business School. He was a nice person and I thought that he could do the mentoring role for us, but he really lacked the process skills to manage the meetings to help us to achieve something. He would help us chat things through, but he was basically a chemist rather than a process consultant, so it was difficult for him because we are fairly advanced in that way and he was not as advanced as we were. We knew him through personal contact: what we had been doing was looking for someone we liked working with and trying them out.

Before that – when I started the business, I was the most experienced one and I took on the development of my partners and they learnt from my experience, so I wanted someone to support me really. Through my contacts, we did a deal with a strategic management consultancy, where they gave us some days' consultancy and we went on some of their courses. The deal was that we would get some support from a person who would structure some sessions for us – he became quite an inspiring figure in helping us along. That was unofficial, though – he played that role with me, personally, also.

It was very interesting when we fell out with this person, because there was no formal relationship. The relationship grew, but then we started to not need him any more. The break-up became very emotional!

So then I looked around for someone else, and I realized that, consciously, I was looking for mentors through the business we were doing. We did a joint project with someone who was very hot on marketing and sales. We developed a mentoring relationship and it went very well initially; but then, again, we fell out in the end, because, I think, the unwritten expectations on either side were not explicit.

Those two experiences, which were really business experiences but which became personal, were both difficult in the end.

After the second one, I began to recognize a pattern and I had some counselling to help me see how I was part of the pattern. I seemed to be looking for a sort of father figure and they saw something in me that they could nurture and I saw something in them that they could provide. The danger is that, as you start to grow, you have an added relationship to contend with, the parent/child, and then rejection is very difficult. And I was obviously looking for people like this.

The important thing was that they were both older than I was and they were both successful consultants and I could see that I could learn from them and they could profit from my energy and my ideas: I think it was a little bit prodigal son and supportive father. That was the dynamic. It became difficult when I tried to make adult-to-adult decisions so that I could learn from them. So for me, the unwritten expectation was that I would learn skills; whereas for them, they were expecting me to be the bright son who always gives them lots of recognition.

If you are to be a mentor, you need to understand this dynamic, because if you are not aware of it, the relationship can become dysfunctional. Unconsciously, your mentee will try to gain your attention by behaving in a dysfunctional way.

So now Tim and I are being mentored together. We have had all our development together so that we're learning what we need as a team.

The two emotional setbacks could have put me off, but I went to a counsellor who helped me to analyse what had happened and I realized that I was set up and that you start getting into games and setting yourself up. And I'm now very wary of who we do projects with. We find it harder to find consultants, because we actually know what we're doing and we have a clear idea of our strategy. We are very independent and we have made our success by being independent.

I mentor people all the time. That is the way we grow in business. I also used to mentor TSB Group's top team, and I do facilitation for the Sheffield TEC executive. In-house, I work with new consultants, giving them support on their projects. We have quarterly performance reviews, and we give people permission to talk in the evenings.

The mentoring is both task and process oriented. We also give feedback – one of our strengths is in giving feedback on interpersonal skills. And you're always a role model. There's always someone they can talk to about how they are doing the things they are doing.

I see my mentoring as being a combination of coach, plus role model, plus someone you can talk to about how well you are doing.

I also mentor some of our customers – there are two at the moment for whom I have been a referee for their MSc at Birkbeck, and I have helped them with that and with their general career, and their personal lives.

I think mentoring is just a part of a general learning by doing. I don't think that it is any different from reviewing your ordinary day-to-day life – it is just having a slightly more removed person to review it. They can stand back a bit more.

Mentors do not need to know your business inside out. They do, however, need to know about some kind of business – so they understand about people and strategy and building relationships. Once you get over the initial level of how do you do marketing and that sort of thing, and business is successful, you need someone who understands the softer issues.

Mentors need to be role models – what we try and do is work out who are successful people, who set goals and achieve goals and who believe that they can do it.

As a mentor in Sheffield TEC, for local businessmen, I have to role model success, confidence, visualizing and achieving. And you must recognize when you are not doing that, because then you will be undermining your mentees' interest. You need to be very positive.

There is a power relationship there – knowledge power and expertise power will be passed on. So, when the mentee is developed enough to move away, they take the power. That's why you need a rational, professional relationship in mentoring, so that these things are understood.

A9   Mike Pupius, Royal Mail: a quality mentor

Mike Pupius was Director of Business Excellence and Planning for Royal Mail North East, and he then took a secondment to the European Foundation for Quality Management in Brussels, responsible for developing a process for promoting business excellence in the public sector throughout Europe.

I have come to mentoring fairly late in my career, but I can pick out five mentors or role models who have influenced me.

The first was Joe Mappin, who I went to when I wanted to sort out my personal fitness and some issues around stress management. He took me up a very steep development curve, which had some interesting outcomes. I went from a low level of fitness to running a half marathon in six months; and running the London marathon in 14 months; then gaining a medal in the World Student Games marathon in Sheffield. A lasting effect is that I continue to do a long run on Sunday mornings, which is also rich in terms of relationship, support and common interest. The relationship with Joe was crucial, especially in the first year, but I also went back to him after I had an operation on my leg and he helped me overcome the fear that, if I ran again, then I might drop down dead. He was there when I needed him, and he was more than a fitness coach – he addressed my lifestyle, the balance in my life, challenging my personal behaviour and my commitment. He became a friend of the family, and it was two-way – we supported him in his business development.

Richard Field is a mentor and a role model. We worked at the same time on getting MPhil degrees. We were both interested in applying Total Quality Management in the community context in Sheffield. Having similar goals led to successful outcomes for both of us. That was two kinds of marathon – the second was a marathon learning experience.

I receive a weekly fax from Richard, though I am not one of his main mentees. I find it helpful; the one-liner to me is very supportive and encouraging. It is something to look forward to and I will be more resolute in sending him weekly updates in return.

My third mentor was my Professor on the MPhil – Gopal Kanji. In the end, of course, I did the dissertation myself, but his being there, chivvying away and challenging my thinking was very worthwhile. I decided to do the MPhil at the time I became Quality Director in Royal Mail North East. It helped me to look outside, in a broader context, and prepared me for challenges I faced in the organization when we came across inevitable pitfalls. The MPhil and Gopal's mentoring helped keep the bigger picture in mind, and has led me to my current position. I have come to see that the EFQM model is a fractal. As well as applying to organizations, it also applies to countries and continents and to individuals. I have also come to recognize through this process that the successful implementation of change is very dependent on managerial behaviour, and that a key role of management is to provide advice, guidance, coaching and mentoring.

The culture of Royal Mail tended to focus more on individual achievement than team performance, which on occasions has led to behaviour not consistent with a TQ focus on people and customers. Nevertheless, my next mentor was in Royal Mail – Ian Raisbeck, the National Quality Director. He maintained a sense of constancy over eight years when I worked first as a District Head Postmaster implementing quality and then as a specialist Director implementing plans. Ian applied the 'current state: future state' model in Royal Mail, and this has done me good not just in the organization but externally when I have worked with schools and small businesses in relationship with the Sheffield community. Ian also gave me an opportunity to visit the United States to benchmark how large organizations became involved in mentoring in the community, especially Corning in New York State and a network of businesses in the city of Erie in Pennsylvania.

My final mentor is my wife, Jenny. She is somebody who listens, challenges and is very supportive. It is a two-way process: I support her business activities, and now her role as the Managing Director of Destination Sheffield.

I act as a mentor to three people. The first is Jill Bungay, a senior officer in Sheffield City Council and a professional Chartered Surveyor. As part of her personal development plan she was placed on a woman's leadership programme, and she had to acquire a mentor. Her boss was one of my Sunday morning running colleagues, and he asked me to do it – initially on a fee-paying basis. I learned about mentoring through doing this with her and there was a lot of background provided by the programme on the process through which we should go.

Six weeks into the relationship she wrote saying that she would terminate the contract as the financial situation had deteriorated, so I contacted. her and said, 'Don't worry, I'll do it without the fee.'

It has now been going for over a year. We started sharing information about each other in terms of Honey and Mumford's learning styles, Myers-Briggs personality styles and also a framework of work styles.

We discuss her course, but also her trials and tribulations in the City Council, which was undergoing change and (in the perception of others) continuous budget crises, downsizing and outsourcing. With a new Chief Executive, it meant staff had to apply for their own or new jobs. A lot of our discussion was about these issues and getting them into perspective. We explored constraints related to union issues, personnel policies and the absence of an appraisal process, and I introduced her to these themes. It culminated in me spending several sessions with her planning a workshop for her staff, where we created a vision statement, identified key issues they faced and planned first actionable steps.

At our most recent meeting, her crunch time had come and we went through preparation for an interview for a job she really wanted – she didn't get it, but came a close second and handled the interview really well. We now have a question about whether the relationship will carry on.

I found that as a mentor I grew and learned together with the mentee. I have learned about problems faced in other organizations; I have built confidence in developing trust in relationships and in simple things like asking questions and providing support.

One improvement I would make in future is to keep a better record of discussions and key points during or after each session – like case notes.

My next mentee is Robert Kirby, who was manager of a hotel in Hong Kong. I shared experience and inspiration with him by fax and e-mail, and then provided him with support in making the transition to a new hotel, which he manages now. I helped him to apply the European Quality model in the new hotel, and contributed to a workshop for his new team at the Hotel Furama.

When I was visiting him, I met my third mentee, Katie, who is a senior manager in a Hong Kong company. As part of a presentation I was doing to the Hong Kong Quality Forum I visited her company and five minutes after we met she was telling me about her difficulties in working with her CEO. I agreed to maintain contact through a series of faxes and subsequently e-mails, offering thoughts and help based on my own experience. I shared presentational material and my organization's material on managing technology, and she has now got over her problem and has come to terms with her situation.

The main input was over the first six months, but a year later it continues, more on the basis of friendship and sharing experiences.

A10 Peer mentoring among managers in the Netherlands by Lida Beers, Hogeschool van Amsterdam, Netherlands

The Renesse group, which started out as a study group and continued as a mentor group, shows us how four very business-like managers are able to offer each other support, advice and a valuable network by discussing questions that relate personality to work.

Ten years ago 22 managers attended a training event called 'The performance of managers', offered by the Foundation of Management Science in Rotterdam. Within the framework of this event, participants worked in subgroups at assignments of a very personal nature. One of these assignments was a highly confronting career management assignment: participants were asked to write, in the group, their own memorial: 'How do you want to be remembered and what are the consequences for the rest of your life?'

The assignment was made even more confronting, because the subgroups were put together according to the so-called 'sociogram method'. Group members were asked to make a choice by taking a position in the room and stand with the persons they preferred; without words, without explaining their motivations. From the start it was clear to the members of one group that they wanted to work with each other. They were four ambitious managers around the age of forty with a strong common drive: to achieve a good career path for the next forty years!

The help they were able to give each other at that point was so useful that they have continued to meet and support each other. The group has even acquired a name – the 'Renesse' group, because they are from the town of Renesse and they are concerned with personal and organizational renaissance. They are all senior executives or directors of their organizations, and continue to ask each other challenging questions about every career step.

I interviewed two members, Joke van Antwerpen and Adrie van Grinsven about their ten-year relationship.

The group

Group members are Henk, at present a manager with AHOLD; Adrie, director of a housing corporation; Eric, director of the Utrecht Academy of Music; and Joke, director of the O&A Consultancy. All four believe that the group being composed of directors of organizations in different sectors is one of its success factors. Although their companies and organizations may have strong differences, there are nonetheless many similarities in processes; consequently much experience can be exchanged – for instance on motivating company members.

Career development as a leading theme

Adrie: One of the assignments in the training event was writing your own 'in memoriam'. That was rather challenging: what will I do for the rest of my life? How do I want to be remembered? What will people say about me and what do I hope they will say about me?

In working with one another on this assignment, we discovered that work dominated our lives. We wanted to discuss what this meant to our attitudes to life.

What are we doing? We are all swallowed by everyday working life and is that what we want?

Joke: It was agreed: we will keep one another to this. When the training ends we will remain together as a group and we will continue to ask each other this same question.

Method

Joke: The group meets with a different member acting as Chair each time. Meetings start on Thursdays at lunch-time and continue till Friday lunch. The heavy agendas of the group members make it ever more difficult to clear so much time, so we have to plan well ahead. The Chair is responsible for the arrangement of accommodation and the programme.

The programme is becoming more and more informal. We always start with an inventory round: how are you? We discuss developments at home and at work. This continues during dinner. Group members ask highly probing questions in response to each other's stories and always make the link to earlier stated intentions.

For our next meeting we have agreed to retrieve career goals that were formulated at an earlier stage. During the meetings we also exchange interesting materials: articles and books which recently proved useful to us as managers or material which we use professionally. For example, I once presented the career orientation test.

Group members can always consult each other between meetings for support and advice. Shared learning experiences often prove to be a meaningful start for discussions.

Adrie: We never have difficulties with picking up the pace, even if we have not met for a long time. Every time, we immediately feel the 'click'.

Learning

Adrie: The specific character of learning in this group is that we allow each other to ask searching questions. This intensity in communication is very positive. There is great willingness to empathize and to invest in each other. But that absolutely does not imply total acceptance or simply trying to please one another, as the aim is to support each other. Because of our busy work schedules we cannot meet very often – but, whenever necessary, we do find the time to meet.

Sometimes you do not hear from someone for a while and then all of a sudden it is necessary to meet. In that case, we have a bilateral meeting; it is not always necessary to meet with all four.

Joke: Being able to discuss things with colleagues of the same stature, who all hold a senior management position, stimulates reflecting on my own management style tremendously. It broadens my horizon. The examples of the others can be very instructive.

Learning climate

Joke: Sharing a long history together helps to create a climate that renders learning possible.

Group members feel safe enough with each other to be allowed, and to be able, to have strong confrontations with one another. In this way group development helps each of us to be really challenging.

Adrie: I consider the group members as stern friends. I can trust them and they will not spare me. What we do exceeds problem-solving. All four of us are prepared to share on terms of some intimacy. One only does that when you feel and know that you don't want to lose one another.

Roles

Joke: I consider all my group members as mentors. Adrie is the most understanding mentor; he has taken upon himself the task of keeping the group together. Most of the time it is Adrie who organizes meetings. Henk is the stern mentor. He is a strong-minded person, most concerned with content, and in his analyses he is the most challenging and confronting of all. Eric is the mentor who keeps group members involved. He has taken upon himself the task of encouraging group members to prepare cases for meetings. He also structures discussions and prepares a paper. As a result of this distribution of roles Henk and I leave it up to the others to make appointments.

Adrie: Joke is our feminine element. She always puts up the question: what makes you tick?

At the same time, she is a very matter-of-fact person. Often she stresses that it is important to seek inner peace – and that one needs to make room for that. Henk is a master sparring partner – he always finds a new and surprising angle. Eric and I are structuring and systematic. Eric puts in the nuance and is very empathetic. I focus on logistics: is this conversation leading us to our aim?

Process

Adrie: At first we had to get used to each other and to discover the spectrum of topics within the group. At the beginning, it really was a voyage of discovery. After that stage I felt: 'This comes in handy, they have the experience, I can ask them.'

Joke: When starting the group, there was a bilateral subgroup within it, which the others did not quite know how to relate to. Now bilateral contacts occur naturally – when necessary, one contacts the group member who will be able to offer the best help. In the beginning, we arranged a meeting including partners, which helped when we discussed our personal lives.

Later, we went through a stage in which we asked ourselves: do we get enough out of this; is it still useful? All of us were extremely busy: appointments were cancelled or people were paged during meetings. So, we linked new subjects to the leading theme.

Adrie: Over the period of the time the group has existed, everybody has taken at least three career steps, but also has had to cope with career frustrations. To date we have had several crises: what will we be doing in five years, what is important? We are all fiftyish now. Everybody is already at the top. Will we be climbing up once more? We have made impressive careers but will we be content when we look back?

Practice

Joke: I presented to the group problems I was having with my own manager, related to the reorganization and the kick-off of O&A

Consultancy. I struggled with whether I still wanted such a demanding job. I felt under great pressure. When I presented my case, the questions from the other group members were so challenging, that I realized almost immediately: 'What we are doing in the O&A group is too desultory. There has to be a change in the way things are managed and communicated to clients.'

As far as my complaint about high work pressure was concerned, I received the feedback: 'You will always be busy, because you always push yourself'.

Adrie: I presented my situation as the director of a housing corporation to the group. I had problems with the Board. It was a power struggle – who was in command? These are thrilling questions: do I accept those higher in command and will I accept the decisions they make? How much room do I allow other people? How can I cope strategically?

In my case discussion in the group helped to straighten things out with the Board. However, this proved to be only a temporary solution. In the end I went looking around: what do I want now? The result is that I have found a new job. In the meantime a lot of bilateral discussion took place with a group member who had had a similar experience.

Results

Adrie: It may be that of all group members Henk is the one who learns the fewest new things. The other three learn a lot from each other. Up to now the group always received a new impulse when one of the members changed jobs, because on such an occasion there is a lot to tell. It may be that within two years we will not change jobs any more and we will not have anything new to discuss. That will be the end.

Joke: In the group we are working very well together. If we continue in this way, we will keep up for another ten years.

A11 Trude Stolpe, Personnel Director, Axel Johnsson, Sweden

This report is based on experiences of the Swedish company Axel Johnsson from a presentation at a workshop during 1998.

We started our mentoring programme four years ago. Antonia Axel Johnsson, our CEO, had spent time in the United States and is very positive about mentoring.

The impetus was a number of seminars around various management issues, one of which was mentoring. We decided that mentoring could be very useful in increasing understanding between levels in the organization and between generations. We asked the University of Stockholm to carry out some initial research and to help us plan the programme.

We started by setting objectives for both mentors and mentees, in discussion with the top team. The key objectives were:

- better understanding between levels
- identify and develop tomorrow's leaders
- exchange of knowledge and experience
- perpetuate the corporate culture.

The mentors were drawn from top management at group headquarters and in the divisions – all operating managers or specialists, not staff people. We looked for people with personal maturity and an interest in developing others. Then we asked the CEO of each division to propose a number of mentees – high flyers typically in their mid-30s. Altogether, we used 12 mentors (out of a pool of 15) for 12 mentees. The pilot was limited to our Swedish operations, although we do have major operations overseas.

Mentees and mentors were each trained over half a day, along with their line managers, so that the latter would understand that the mentors were not there to interfere in line issues and that it would sometimes be necessary for the mentee to disappear for a meeting with the mentor.

Mentors were given a self-assessment questionnaire to provide a profile, against which mentees could select. Mentees were given a questionnaire to help them define what sort of person they were looking for, then a set of mentor profiles. The mentees were then responsible for informing the mentor of their choice.

All of this took three months, in the last six weeks of which either party could duck out, before the relationship formally started. In the twelve months since the formal start-up, we have run a series of training programmes to help the process along. These have included seminars or workshops on communication skills, gender issues and leadership.

After six months, we brought the mentors together again to review progress. We also did the same with mentees, who became a very tightly focused team. We found that relationships with a male mentor and female mentee worked best and that the most difficult issues for the group(s) were finding the time to meet and geographical separation. We have now launched a second programme, along the lines of the first.

One relationship involved a very beautiful woman and a 55-year-old man. There was a lot of negative comment and misconceptions when they met in the evening. It was an issue that participants really needed to think about.

Mentor profile

We advised mentees to look for a mentor who is:

- interested in others
- a good listener
- confident in themselves
- a good networker
- able to maintain the separation between their role as mentor and the line manager's development role
- experienced in business and the business
- ready to learn.

Evaluation

Mentors' and mentees' evaluations of the programme were very positive.

A12   Allen Yurko, CEO, Siebe – an American story

A senior director talks about a series of mentors who were prominent leaders in the companies where he has worked.

I think the most important mentors, and ones that should never be forgotten, are parents. My parents have been a guiding light for me in my whole life, my father particularly on the business side. He was a successful businessman, an entrepreneur, who started his own business in high technology electronics and exposed me to business as a very young man. He taught me at an early age, say 13–15 years old, to help out on weekends and evenings. Later on, during university, I spent summers working at his factory on the assembly line. Not a very big factory, maybe 200 employees, but I was given a direct flavour very quickly of what business was all about – what made money and what didn't make money. He never treated me with kid gloves. He would put me anywhere that he had a problem, and people would work a little harder.

My mother, although not highly educated, was very much a proponent of education. As I look at all of our family I can see the same thing – a high achievement mentality – and I think a lot of that came from my mother. She was always there to help me get through college, get started and find my own way. When I graduated from college I didn't know what I wanted to do. I had a job offer of being a golf professional and another as an accountant. My father said, 'It's totally up to you – I'm leaving on vacation for two weeks. When I get back I want you to have a job.' I was on my own – which was fine – and made the decision to go into accounting. The relationship with my parents was one that was certainly strong: they have always been a guiding light, supportive.

Having a tough but fair and loving relationship with my father made it easier for me to accept criticism from others, to understand the difference between negative criticism and coaching or mentoring. I think that as a result of this, later on in my career I was able to fall more easily into more unstructured situations. I was getting a little more coaching, counselling and direction than the average executive because I wanted it, and, because I was accepting the extra coaching, the other person felt more comfortable giving.

I think parental mentoring carried me through the first five or six years of my career. During that time I never had a boss for more than 18 months. My career was moving along so quickly there was not time for anyone to put me under their wing. It would have been nice to have had one, but there was so much change, and not much time.

My first big mentor in business came when I joined Joy Manufacturing in 1978. By that time I had been out of education five and a half years and had become an assistant controller for the largest division of Joy Manufacturing in the coal mining equipment business. There was an executive there named Carl Heinz who was the group vice president. I think in the early days there I was in direct interface with him on only three or four occasions per month and I believe he liked my approach to business. This was a very successful company. One of the reasons I had left my previous job to go to Joy was because Joy was the leading division of that kind in the world and I wanted to see how this was achieved. Carl Heinz was the man, in my opinion, who had built the strategy, implemented the strategy and was taking all the decisions to make it continue. Over three to four years we structured a loose mentor relationship which involved Mr Heinz overseeing my career steps and the assignments I was given. It was not day-to-day mentoring, but at critical times and at all key meetings where he and I were present, he would ensure that my opinion was sought.

He was the major proponent for me to become the youngest division controller in Joy Manufacturing's history (and in the biggest division making much of the corporation's profit). I was only 28 years old. He totally supported me with the Group's CFO (who appreciated that I was a good young talent but I don't think was necessarily ready to give me the division controllership). He, as group vice president, was saying I was ready, and he carried a lot of weight. I had been with them for a couple of years at that time. I had several other champions supporting the decision, so in the end I did become the youngest division controller in Joy history.

I think the most important point was that I had taken some risks during my first two years there and made some radical changes to the cost accounting system that had resolved significant problems. Previously unidentified variances were being identified and once you identify something you can begin to manage it; once you have managed it and have fixed it, you see bottom-line results. I also spent a lot of time on the shop floor. I was not just sitting behind a bunch of balance sheets – I was actually out there on the floor and doing my homework.

The relationship with Carl Heinz was based on business. We did, however, have a little bit more of a personal relationship. We occasionally played golf together. We didn't talk business on the golf course much because I was two levels below him. He felt that it would have been unfair to my boss for him to be going direct to me. If there was some overriding business issue that everyone was talking about, we got into that, so there was some general business discussion. However, it was mainly just quality time.

I think one of the toughest decisions I made was to take a job that would only come along once in a lifetime. I felt very bad about leaving the relationship I had with Joy. On the other hand, I had made a lot of contributions: the company was in a very good state; the issues that I had come to resolve were close to being resolved. My career was still embryonic at the time. I think that when you move up the ladder as fast as I did, often the compensation does not keep up. You get very healthy pay increases but your value on the market rises more quickly than what you are getting paid. I had not been put on a stock option plan or anything like that. So when those kind of things were offered to me by a business that was two and half times the size, and very international, I decided to leave Joy. Carl tried to get me to stay. He worked to understand the reasons why I was leaving, and I basically went through the financial side of it – young man interested in building a career and getting double the money. Joy made an attempt at keeping me, and I really did want to stay for a lot of reasons, but eventually I took the other job.

I didn't find a mentor there and maybe that is why I decided to leave two years later. But I think the real reason was that I felt I needed a different kind of challenge. I was becoming less and less enchanted with big business because of its bureaucracy and slowness in decision-making. I was getting frustrated with it, so I thought I ought to try something else, another level of business, more entrepreneurial.

I left Eaton and went to Mueller, a small $200 million valve manufacturer in the mid-West. It was run by my next great mentor, Ed Powers, who was CEO there. He had been trained in the tough Harold Geneen school at ITT. He was an entrepreneur who had left ITT so that he could run a more fast-paced yet tightly controlled organization. I liked his style – it was tough, no nonsense. You just knew that if you needed his support, he would give it to you. I joined a small team that was expanding the company aggressively. Ed was someone who could provide mentoring in a more entrepreneurial way, in a fast-paced business environment, with a degree of toughness and that worked for me. I stayed with Mueller for six years. The management team, with the support of several investment banks, eventually bought the company about three and a half years after I joined. We raised $5 million and borrowed $295 million. That was an exciting time. Ed had helped me to recognize that I needed more shop floor and business acumen so he worked hard to get me into operations. Actually, in the early years before we bought the company, he assigned me the job of being vice president of the Canadian operation. So at the same time as being CFO of this company, I was also vice president of the Canadian operation. That was a direct attempt to get me operating responsibility and it worked well – we did a good job.

When we bought the company, he said, 'Right, you have done the Canadian thing, time to come back and help us through this leveraged buy-out.' I spent my time back in the centre, putting the LBO together, getting bank finance and then running it for two years or so. The deal worked. The buy-out worked. It was a difficult time for our market but nevertheless the company continued to generate cash and a few years later we decided to sell it to Tyco International. Unfortunately, Ed decided to retire and I couldn't come to terms with this so I started looking for another job. It was a little scary. I had made some money on the stock, but was jobless for the first time in my career.

That was when I met my fourth and final mentor, Barrie Stephens. I didn't feel like getting back into corporate America – I had had 8–10 years of it. I met directly with Barrie Stephens and his management board. I said, 'That's the CEO I want to work for.' I think since the time that I went to Joy, whenever I moved on, it would be an individual I was going to work for, the person was running the organization, not necessarily my. direct boss, who I was really choosing, as opposed to wanting to work for this or that company. I didn't know anything about Siebe. All I had was an hour and ten minute interview with Barrie Stephens.

The meeting was in Florida. There were six people interviewing me but the only executive doing the talking was Barrie Stephens. I think we hit it off immediately. He was actually hiring the vice president of finance for Siebe's Robertshaw subsidiary and that was a job I knew I could do. I asked him a couple of core questions – what is the future possibility at Siebe to move into operations? I understood that he wanted me to come in and prove myself by running the financial side of Robertshaw, but I wanted the longer-term opportunity of moving into operations and being general manager or president. He gave me the answer I needed most. If I did well, operations was a distinct possibility. That's what happened. I always felt he was somebody I could talk to, could share not only my strategies and my plans with but also my concerns. He would help sort them out, in other words give me verification that I was heading in the right direction. Even in that first interview, he led me to believe that my desired career path was the right one and that Siebe was the right company to join to do it. He was very emphatic about that, so confident and so quick in the decision that at the end of the interview he essentially offered me the job.

I think each of my mentors contributed something different in building my management style. My father demonstrated a very strong achievement style; closeness and openness; the value of a lot of quality time together between people that need to get along. My father made sure he made time for all of us. So that was the personal side, but there was also a tough side. You knew if you got out of line then there would be a more direct approach that followed.

Carl Heinz was clearly the best team builder that I have ever worked for. I had come from a business that had gone through constant re-engineering and restructuring. Here was a successful executive running this equipment mining business that was doing things like advanced human resource development, team building, on the shop work teams. This was back in the 1970s and was very advanced for the time. He had installed a training department to train and build upon the engineering and technical skills and also the human resource of a classic 'Theory Y' environment. It was working. I came from a culture of: I'm the boss, let's work things through but at the end of the day, we are going to do it my way. This was more collaborative, team building. I valued just seeing a successful business running – the kind of investment that was being made, R&D, the growth mentality of it as opposed to a restructuring mentality.

When I went to Mueller, we had to achieve a turnaround, so there was an absolute focus on the bottom line. It was also very people-oriented, but not from a human resource development approach – more let's do it through the infrastructure that exists, through the power structure and through the organization. Ed Powers brought a 'I will not be denied, we will achieve' approach. He built a very strong senior management team. It was a close-knit group. He kept it close – we met when we needed to. It was an informal management style, but you knew you would be there when you should be part of the decision-making process. It was an absolute myopic approach to business: 'We are going to win – it's just a matter of time. We are going to achieve this objective. If we get it wrong, we do it again till we get it right.' I had never before seen that aggressive approach to hitting targets and achieving the numbers. In my days at Joy we were driven, but not to this level. The other pieces were there but it was this 'can do, will do, must do' attitude that was truly the thing I gained from my years with Ed Powers.

Barrie Stephens brought a combination, which continues today, of that same 'must do' attitude and a focus on building an international presence. He achieved both through involvement. Again there was heavy emphasis on training, development, building of a strong base of people, but also on building an exceptionally fast decision-making process. Watching Barrie Stephens for years as I came up the ladder, I saw him make decisions daily which other corporations of the same size would have taken months over. He would make a decision based on how well people had done their homework and whether they could deliver what they promised.

I tried to structure a couple of mentor relationships in my early years at Eaton, though I couldn't say that at the time I knew how to do this. Just because of the nature of the business one of my potential mentors was swept away and promoted so I had no contact with him. I think he had developed the early signs of being a mentor for me and after only a few months he was gone. The second time around I tried to find a mentor relationship but I was unable to find anyone. I think we were under too much pressure. We were just trying to do so many things so fast – I just don't think the business environment was right for it. Maybe the people were not right either.

The strongest direct mentoring came from Barrie Stephens – there I had a direct one-on-one relationship with someone I considered to be my mentor and without question it was quality one-on-one time, either on the phone or face-to-face, talking about the issues . . . clarity of vision and clarity of direction were central to all of those discussions. The giving and receiving of feedback on my performance was not in a structured format but weekly, monthly, sometimes daily, whenever it should and could come up. I did not have to wait for a formal performance review at the end of the year: I knew how I was doing. This was the style. If you were off track, you were going to know today. You also knew when you were on track and doing a good job. All of my mentors were very liberal with their praise – it wasn't just negative feedback. Also they brought me in on all the critical decision-making points – I felt part of the team.

I think that in all cases we chose each other. It was not a question of my mentor being similar to myself, but definitely I thought I could emulate these people. I just felt a sense of urgency about them, a sense of running the business the way I thought by that time in my career was the right way to do it. So I was working with a mentor, who I thought I would like to emulate.

Without question the values of my mentors were generally the same – the intensity they brought to the business, how they made decisions on people quickly and nourished and empowered the best ones and, when there was someone that unfortunately wasn't working out, they made the change quickly. This was never in a negative and hurtful way, but in a spirit of 'let's get it done (it's in everybody's best interests) and move on.' They had strong values for the shareholders and stakeholders in the company. There were the core values of customers and quality, building the business from the ground up as opposed to just going through a series of acquisitions and turnarounds and ending up with a lot of businesses. They had a growth mentality. All those values were what I saw.

I have thought about me as a mentor – how much mentoring have I really done? I would say that during my career I have done some mentoring. I know that there is least one man here at Siebe who I mentor and that is working very well. It's a similar relationship. He reports to the CFO, not to me, so I often work through his boss. At other times I work directly with him, though only because he goes with me to a lot of meetings off-site. I would say that once again the mentoring is informal – he may not even agree he is being mentored.

Earlier in my career, I certainly did some other mentoring even less formally. I also had very good executives who still to this day call me for advice. I have five or six of those who have stood the test of time for up to 15 years now, people who have stayed close to me. There was a sufficiently strong mentoring relationship maybe ten years ago that when they were given the opportunity to come to Siebe, they said yes.

One-on-one time doesn't have to be long, but it has to be quality. I think you need to talk about the basic values. The mentees have to sense that you are giving constructive feedback. I definitely work hard at being positive, though it is not the easiest thing for a mentor to do – you tend to be hardest on someone you want to perform to a higher level. You have such high expectations that you tend not to see the smart things they do along the way. Maybe you don't stroke them as much as someone you are a little more worried about.

I encourage all our CEOs to put someone under their wings. They tend to talk about that person more than others, coach them, guide them, yes, mentor them.

# A13	Kees Zandvliet, HRM Director, Heineken, Netherlands: a functional director is professionally mentored – by Nina Lazeron

In this case a director responsible for a major function is being mentored by an external specialist in that function. The mixing of mentoring and professional advice seems to weaken the relationship. An informal mentor is more long-lasting and rewarding.

When I accepted my present position I realized the importance of asking various colleagues for advice on which steps I could take that would be of benefit and help to me. One trusted colleague suggested taking a mentor from outside Heineken, somebody who would serve the purpose of a mirror for myself, someone I could reflect my personal and professional dilemmas with. I immediately thought of someone who stuck out in my mind, who I thought could fill this role, and who had played this role before in a complex professional situation. Unfortunately, they were too busy at the time to take on this task but recommended someone else to me. And so it came to be that I met with my recommended consultant once a month for a couple of hours over lunch.

In my opinion, the qualities I am looking for in a mentor are somebody who radiates a sense of tranquillity and the ability to listen. He must have a real interest in people, someone who is not necessarily old but still carries his share of grey hairs built up from his own experiences and revelations in life. My mentor must be able to feel and recognize emotions. I do not think that it was particularly necessary for my mentor to have a Human Resource Management background, though in my case it did turn out to be handy. Not only is it an important quality for a mentor to have plenty of listening ability, they must also be blessed with the ability to go into a trusted depth of understanding.

The things we work on are, for instance, my professional situation and my own analysis of this situation, the way the management looks upon the changing situation of the company, and the internal functioning of the management team. But we also discuss more personal items like, how does one present oneself, what is one's contribution and role within the team one is working in, among both colleagues and employees, and the instruments one needs in one's work. By talking with my mentor I learned to see the strong and weak points within our team and this taught me to focus on the future role and abilities of our Human Resource Management work. This was how we would deal with the professional side of things, but we also discussed the way I cope with stress and how to keep a balance between my personal and professional life. I had to learn how to make priority choices and then learn how to stick to them.

So in the beginning, the confidence between my mentor and I had to grow. During this period it was absolutely necessary that we had a complete feeling of trust and confidentiality.

My mentor and I never became personal friends. The relationship stayed professional, even though the personal and professional items we discussed varied over a broad range. Because he was also a Human Resource Consultant, he was able to help me with practical ideas and connections in the line of work. Our relationship became less and less important and over a period of time the necessity to meet started to diminish. During this time, a colleague of his came to help develop my department, and partly took over the role he used to have, especially the professional part.

I have learned a lot, and I do use my acquired wisdom on mentoring whenever I talk to my workers. The conscious level of communication is important – I mean that there is more to talk about than just work! I learned to pay attention not only to the business aspects: personal aspects count for a lot and need taking care of too. Sometimes I do advise people to take a mentor, especially if they have to make decisions about their future career. When a person gets stuck then there is a mismatch between the way the environment looks at them and the way they look at themselves. A mentor will provide you with a mirror, a way of reflecting yourself, which can be confronting. It would be preferable if we could do this with each other inside the company, but I do question the possibilities of this. A mentor from outside probably has an easier, less emotional starting point.

I sometimes mentor others, and I am convinced that it would be hard to become a good mentor if you have never felt what it means to be mentored yourself. It is an experience, a very personal feeling of being coached and helped.

Going back to the first person who I thought of as 'my' mentor (the one who did not have the time), he still is the one who I see as a real mentor to me. I have known him for a long time, and whenever we meet we question and confront each other thoroughly and profoundly. During the first years that we knew each other, this mentor used to confront me and we had a kind of master–pupil relationship, but then after two years we reached a new balance.

If you would ask me who I would call when I am in trouble, it would be this person, the one who first stuck out in my mind, and I know he would be there for me. We do not meet very often but I know that if we needed each other we would always be there. So it is not just about friendship, there is an added special something. Call it a kind of magnetism, being able to click with someone – call it compassion – call it mentoring!

B1 Julia Essex, mentored by Ian Flemming: one mentor – several organizations

B1a Julia Essex, Director of Commissioning, East Hertfordshire Health Service

Julia Essex has made a number of rapid moves to a Directorship of a Health Service Trust. She has had a professional mentor who has provided continuity in steering her career and developing herself.

My mentor, Ian Flemming, is a paid external advisor. He has been my mentor for six years through jobs in three organizations. In the first, I paid him myself; in the second two, the organization has paid for his 'tutoring', which is seen as 'high value' development for me. Initially it was quite difficult to explain and justify this, as the concept of mentoring was an unfamiliar approach to personal development in the Health Service. It is more popular now.

As well as giving me personal advice, Ian lends me books and tapes which are self-supporting development materials, so I go away with something interesting to do – the process is not wholly introspective. We meet three or four times a year, usually about a specific issue and initiated by me when I need it. When things are going fine there have been quite big gaps.

I see mentoring as different from other relationships at work in that: it is essentially long-term; it concerns both work and personal issues; it addresses balance in the mentee's life; and it is based on the mentee's agenda.

You get the greatest benefit from a long-term relationship because this becomes increasingly effective as you do not have to keep re-explaining things. You need an empathy with the mentor – I don't wear my heart on my sleeve, it takes a while for my feelings to emerge. When they do, though, it is highly beneficial to talk about complex and sometimes emotive issues at work without feeling vulnerable.

Issues we have addressed include leadership, delegation, and my tendency to be a 'power freak'. We have not looked at my role on the Board, or at becoming a Board member, because this has been dealt with through Organization Development work within the organization.

I met Ian six years ago when he ran a series of three courses on personal development that I found particularly useful. At the time of the last one, my job changed significantly in a way which was not of my choosing. Ian was very helpful in talking this through, and the individual mentoring started from there. There was a clear issue for us to focus on – rebuilding my confidence – and I valued Ian's experience outside the NHS. I believe this gave him a much wider range of experiences than those I had gone through.

I have seen a couple of other people in a sort of mentoring capacity, including an organizational 'bereavement counsellor', provided by an NHS organization, to help deal with a major and unexpected restructuring. They were helpful and specific, but because of my long-term relationship with Ian, I did not need them for long.

Ian has had a broader focus – on all aspects of me as an individual – and has given me personal coping mechanisms, so that, for example, I could use unwelcome change as an opportunity to make choices and to move on.

He has helped me to think about my CV and what I have to offer an organization and how I might express this. He would coach me on interview questions and ask, 'Do you realize what you said?', and help me to develop a strong interview style. In terms of outcomes, I had a 90 per cent success rate in getting interviews and 50 per cent success in being offered posts. He has also helped in other aspects of my life, to gain a balance between work and non-work activities.

I have needed to look at my personal behaviour and skills in dealing with difficult relationships. He was objective and helped me to analyse a problem and look at a range of options. We were able to be very focused on the issues that we wanted to address, which suited my learning style – if someone encourages me to be really specific about a problem, I find that helpful.

I got into choppy waters in entering the current job two and a half years ago. Three days before I was due to take up the post, the Chief Executive rang and warned me of an impending restructuring which could imply the removal of the post. I phoned Ian, who calmed me down and helped me to express my concerns in a positive way. He helped me to handle a very difficult situation positively.

His help has also been valuable for me in my helping others to cope with these kinds of changes. He talked me through the issues for them in the same sort of way as we had done for me: 'What is the problem? What are the options for change?'

Inevitably there have been some tensions in our relationship – at one time he tried to get me angry with him as I have difficulty expressing anger, and that irritated me! Sometimes I finish a session thinking, 'How dare he?', but by the time I am half-way down the motorway, I am saying, 'Damn it, he's right; I need to make a decision on that.' It is a big benefit to me to know that if I have a particular problem I can ring him up, even if I don't do it very often.

He has said that being a mentor is rewarding for him and has extended the range of help he can provide. He has the patience of Job, which is an important quality.

It is highly desirable for directors to have a mentor, because in a senior position it is difficult to seek independent advice without worrying about being able to share personal feelings of incompetence. Among my colleagues, most people have found someone that they can use in this way.

I have supported one of the people who I manage, who has suffered similar disruptions to me and a series of moves that felt like demotions. I have worked with her to give her a broad range of responsibility to help her to present a balanced CV, and, on the mentoring side, I have been supporting her as a colleague, helping her to think through the radical change she has been through. She is now in a supportive, structured learning set, which gives her wider exposure. My being mentored has helped me to help her, by Ian acting as a role model, but also because he provided sound advice in how to handle the difficulties I face in this relationship.

B1b   Ian Flemming, Julia's mentor, is a partner in Ian Flemming Associates

My relationship with Julia is both formal and informal. It is formal in the sense of my trying to get some clarity from her about what her agenda is before she arrives. It is also paid, and we work to strict time boundaries. It also has informal qualities, as we are friendly, and I like her.

I have become a mentor because it is one of the things I know that I am good at, and I go into it with confidence. That does not apply to all I do, so it gives me great satisfaction.

I have no expectations or fears about the relationship – it could continue or it could end; it is up to her to decide – that is part of the deal of mentoring.

We talk about a very wide range of issues, including much around the balance of her life. I would typically challenge her about working ridiculous hours or not taking care of herself. Sometimes I am very confronting; sometimes I draw her out and help her to build her commitment to something. I get her to draw diagrams of situations as she sees them.

I prepare for the meetings by having a phone call with Julia on what she wants, which I will mull over. Then I offer a plan for the meeting, which she may modify.

We are similar, in that we both have power drives – but we express them in different ways. Julia's wish to carry on is what keeps the relationship going. I do not experience any problems in the relationship – it feels like a piece of work I do, but it is also very pleasant to see Julia. I don't talk about it much, but when I do mention it anonymously, I refer to it as a mentoring relationship.

The limits of the relationship are set by what we both see to be valuable. We would not talk about some aspects of her personal life, but we would talk about relationship issues – feelings that might go right back. I stretch the process of what we do – for example when I got her to be angry with me. She found that uncomfortable. I do not talk about my own difficulties; I put those to one side when I am with Julia.

A critical issue we discussed early on was her relationship with her ex-husband, and how that related to her commitment to her own career. She has changed out of all recognition since the beginning. This is not as a result of the mentoring – she has done it herself. This has reinforced my appreciation of difference: you do not have to have the same values to have a helpful relationship.

I would not change the approaches I have used with Julia over the years, because they reflected how I was then. I would handle some of the issues differently if I encountered them now, because I am learning myself. I work in quite an intuitive way – I don't prepare for mentoring in the way I do for running a course. Perhaps I should.

I have also helped her outside the mentoring relationship – I have worked with her team a bit; she's given me advice about the NHS for other work I have done; we have had some really nice lunches together.

I think that mentoring is particularly useful for directors because of their tendency to be seduced by their own power. They can have unrealistic self-belief, and not see their impact on others. They are isolated, and need people who will stand up to them. From time to time I tell another of my mentees that he is arrogant, and, as part of an overall process, he has found this useful.

B2 Michael Fowle, KPMG – voluntary cross-sector mentoring of headteachers

Michael Fowle is a partner in KPMG, and Business in the Community Mentor of the Year.

I mentor both headteachers and people in KPMG, though the in-company mentoring is generally informal. Before, I had never thought about it much, and had not even used the term. I did get into a book on coaching some years ago – I bought 500 and distributed them around the company. I found that mentoring and coaching were done more in the places where it was least talked about.

One thing that sets aside people who survive here into their 40s and make a success of their careers is that they get picked up by mentors when they are in their 20s. The key for junior partners is to get a more senior partner to be their mentor. It is more difficult to enter into a mentoring relationship when you are more senior, because you see other senior managers as a threat, as competition. I am not a political character, so I find it less of a problem.

Teaching is also very political, even in the staffrooms of primary schools. The staff need someone to talk to, someone who is not their boss. One of my mentees has now found a manager in Shell to mentor her deputy, who has found the relationship very beneficial.

KPMG started headteacher mentoring after I went on a 'Seeing is believing' visit to two schools, organized by Business in the Community. I was both impressed and depressed by what I saw. The idea of providing business consultants as mentors to headteachers had been around for a while, but we were the first to take it on.

Headteachers enter the profession to teach, but they end up running a big business, dealing with customers, suppliers, human resource problems, finance and a lot more besides. Often, the last person they can talk to is the chairman of the Board of Governors, who is their boss and can fire them. But they can usefully talk once a month to an intelligent businessperson, who understands the same sort of issues.

We piloted the scheme with 15 schools in year one, 40 in year two. Now we have 450 mentoring relationships, involving lots of companies, and we are aiming for 5000 by the millennium.

The kind of people we look for are open and sensible, at least 30, with practical experience. The schools we selected to begin with were all inner-city – all but one are still with the scheme. It is not necessary that the mentor is more senior than the mentee in age or experience. But they do have to be able to listen, to bring outside perceptions, to give advice from a different perspective and build personal chemistry.

My mentee has 10 teaching staff and seven administrative staff, plus contractors, such as catering. Her problems are remarkably similar to mine. However, if I have a problem, I have 300 partners to call on – she has to depend largely on her own resources. I can sack partners; for her, it is a horrendous problem to fire a poor teacher, even though they may have a serious effect on a generation of youngsters. She talks to me about issues in the school, about dealing with parents, or with neighbouring schools. She books the appointments.

Once she rang me up to ask if I could give her an hour that day. She had been asked by the local education authority and the diocese (hers is a Church school) to take a secondment at another school whose headteacher had been fired. She had considered all the issues but one – how would it affect her career and what was in it for her? She had looked at the problem as one of duty, rather than of commercial opportunity. She had just never thought that way. When she went back to the authority, she got a substantial bonus to reward her for taking on the additional responsibility.

We don't have to talk about financial issues, because she is on top of them – she is very clearly focused on cash flow. That is not typical of headteachers. We have talked a lot about relationships with governors. She is on very good terms with hers – again not always the case in other schools – but she needs to talk through how she manages them. The governors in state schools have a great deal of executive authority – headteachers cannot expel unruly students on their own, for example.

There are no boundaries to what we discuss. I take responsibility for nothing. As soon as you take responsibility, you become a manager or co-manager. As soon as you have any formal standing, it becomes difficult to talk openly.

In return for helping her think these things through, she helps me think through my issues. I find it enjoyable; I'm never quite sure what she gets out of it. I don't think she will progress to another mentor. Our relation-ship will evolve naturally into one where we just keep in touch.

Another headteacher, this time of a tough school in King's Cross, with all the inner city, multi-racial issues, found mentoring useful in helping her look at how she dealt with her time. She was dealing with crises all the time, never having the space to plan major improvements. Her mentor – a woman who is very organized personally – persuaded her to employ two or three more staff to handle crises and take the first brunt of problems. It gave her the breathing space to change the school.

B3 Dame Rennie Fritchie: a top manager role model

Dame Rennie has been Chair of the South West Regional Health Authority (with a £3.4 billion budget), she is Honorary Professor of Creative Leadership at the University of York, the first non-medical President of the British Association of Medical Managers, and a Member of the General Medical Council.

There are two popular songs that relate to mentoring – one: 'You are the wind beneath my wings'; and the other (with slight amendment to the words): 'Anything I can do, you can do better'. My experience of mentoring is that sometimes I help someone with a broken wing to rest and recover and sometimes I help them to soar higher.

I am conscious of the meaning derived from the Greek story of the mentor as 'wise advisor'. I see mentors as attending to other people in their current situation and fostering their future potential by taking a warm (more than professional) interest in the whole person. It is a responsive role, in that you do not go out to do it to people – they tend to ask for it. I do not know what the other person needs to explore or how I can be useful, and often at the start neither do they. The initial role is to set the tone and create a climate where both can agree a purpose for the relationship. It is not a cosy role and, while simple in concept, it is complex in practice, evolving uniquely in each case. The relationship is like weaving a Fairisle sweater – looking equally harmonious on both sides, and all the colours fitting with each other. It is a holistic process.

My first experience of being mentored was when I was 13. I had a road accident and was in hospital for months. My English teacher, Miss Blackman, supported me. She came and brought me work and kept me up to date with what was going on at school. What makes me see this as mentoring is that I felt picked out, that she had made me special – I felt that she recognized some bit of me that had potential, and that might not get developed unless it was attended to. This helped me to value the potential myself.

I met my next mentor when I went as a young wife with small children to America. She was called Opal Montgomery, and she was a grandmother who lived next door. She put me wise to much about living in another culture, about marriage, life and how to do things. She did it in a folksy sort of way; she was not a soft comforter, she was matter-of-fact, down-to-earth, and she used stories to help me see the best in people. She took me under her wing.

In my professional life I have only had one mentor – Mario van Berschoten, who, for the first couple of years that I worked in training and development, gave me half a day every four months. I have returned this gift and always mentor someone as gift work – currently I am mentoring three people in this way.

I also engage in co-mentoring with a small group of three people, meeting for half a day every two months. Our process is to catch up with what we have done since the last meeting, to then explore a particular theme, and to help each other work through things related to the theme. We have decided to spend a year on each theme and are currently exploring endings and death. This group emerged from a biography group, which met for eight or nine years.

In the period between Mario mentoring me and the recent formation of the group (Mario is a member of this too), I cannot recall having a mentor in my work life. In the words of Antony Machado, 'You make the way as you go, traveller; there is no path; only foam paths in the sea'. I have always been travelling new paths, which is why I feel I have a responsibility to people with a difference. I can validate them as they are, and also help them with understanding of the political field, where being right is never enough.

When I was surrounded by the 'Circumference of Sirs', which is what I called the other Chairs of Regional Health Trusts, I felt alone not only as the only woman, but also because all the other Chairs had been captains of industry before joining the NHS. I suggested to one that, 'I think that we two should meet separately and discuss issues that concern us.' He said he would check it out with the others. Later he came back to me and said, 'Rennie, if you have any problems, you can come to any of us with them.' He was unable to see the value of mutual trust and vulnerability, although six months later the Chairs did propose we had 'strategy meetings' to discuss issues. For these relationships to work, what is needed is sharing of your life, being vulnerable, knowing that the other will respect this, and that they will not try to apply their answers to your situation.

I have learned a lot with the help of friends such as Val Hammond, the head of Roffey Park Management College, but that is not mentoring – we have never named it as such.

I have also learned a lot during visits to New Zealand about the Maori way of being an elder. Older Maori women have formed 'language nests' where they keep the traditions alive by teaching the language and telling the stories which carry the learning of the old times. They also have a process whereby, if someone is going for a new job and you are asked to give a reference, you go along with them to the interview, and stand up and speak for them, being duty bound to tell everything. If the applicant gets the job, their old colleagues will bring them to the new workplace on the first day, so they are woven in to the new community, and their new colleagues know their friends from the old one. The Maoris believe that wisdom resides in the elders – they are revered and appreciated, and when they speak they start by talking about their own ancestors: 'These are the people who stand behind me.' The old people are there to catch the young if they fall, to stand behind them, to push them forward. Old people help the young to touch tomorrow, to go forward into the future. The old expect to have something to teach. I remember an old man who was distressed because he felt that he had nothing to teach his grand-children because they were into computer graphics. Then, when they went into business on their own account, he was happy, because he had experience of business and could tell them stories about this.

I started mentoring in Marks and Spencer. I ran training events for managers who had reached a plateau, and these sometimes led to mentoring relationships. Nowadays most of my mentoring is done in the NHS – or with those seeking to enter it. Recently I have been helping an Air Vice-Marshal, who wants to learn the stories that are told in the NHS before he applies for a big NHS job.

I helped the NHS Women's Unit to provide executive coaching for women, because it was felt that they were not getting top jobs because they behaved differently from men, and they did not know this. I was asked to provide up to three days' mentoring in half-day sessions every other month. I keep a notebook of what they say they will do at each meeting and we review this at the start of the next. The aim is not for them to behave like men but to recognize how they act and to make conscious choices about this.

With some women from the Women's Unit, I run a three-day workshop, followed by a half-day one-to-one, with a video camera focused on them as they talk; this demonstrates how they come over. They take the tape away, but often this has led to them seeking an ongoing mentoring relationship.

I work with a duo of the Chairman and the Chief Executive of an NHS Trust, where I meet them both separately and together, and among other things we work on their relationship.

When I was Chair of the South and West Region people would ask, 'Can I shadow you? I want to see what it is like up there, and you seem approachable.' Following this they would seek a de-brief, asking, 'Why did you do it in this way?', and I would say what the context was. I like to have a process by which I can give wise advice, and explain what kind of person I am, so they can see why I have this particular range of choices. One woman asked to shadow me for three months as part of a develop-ment programme she was on. We have agreed she will shadow me during the work I do for one organization I work with, and the rest of the time she will be involved with that organization doing work herself. She is one of many where the decision to seek a mentor has been taken in a moment – they say, 'I need to get to know this woman; she has things that I want to know, although just yet I don't know what they are.'

I mentor a Chief Executive on an ongoing basis who tells me in really positive terms how much seeing the view from another pair of eyes has changed his practice. My experience is that these changes can involve 'bold strokes or the long march', in Rosabeth Moss Kanter's words. Sometimes the change is sharp, but at other times it emerges from walking with them for a while in this stage of their journey.

One relationship which did not work well was with a woman who worked for an organization where I respected the leaders, and I took her on for them. She seemed jolly and outgoing, but when I asked her what her goals were for the mentoring she included my 'being her friend'. I find this is not a part of the professional relationship of mentoring – especially if it is being paid for. With friends both parties take time to deal with their own matters. In this relationship she became very needy, and I felt overwhelmed after our sessions. She wanted advice, connections, friendship, therapy, a mother. I decided to let the relationship go.

It is important to agree a contract at the beginning, about how much you are going to act as a sounding board or a speaking partner, how much you will challenge or support. In one relationship with a General Manger of an organization I chair I was told, 'Your job is to support me. I want now to be carried by someone who does not want anything from me.' This initial contract can change over time, of course.

Every relationship is different, but the mentor is in charge of facilitating the process. Within each meeting, we usually start with a catch-up, where they talk about what they have done since the last meeting. Then I talk for a short time about what has been happening to me, so there is some reciprocity without me using the time to deal with my own issues. Then we identify a theme: 'What would you like today to be about?' We explore what they want from me related to this theme, and then we work upon it. The mentor's job is to attend to this agreement, the purposes, boundaries, processes and benchmarks and to restate them if things go too far off track or become erratic.

Over a mentoring relationship the process often begins with *reflection*. I ask people to tell me their life story, and I tell a bit of mine (which avoids the risk of it feeling like voyeurism). I am seeking not what they come with that day, but who this person is – the picture out of which they have stepped. My role is to be wholly present for them. This way I get their temperament, their hesitancies. This can take a couple of hours, and out of that time I will spend a few minutes telling them about my biography – as a sort of pump-priming process. The aim is not to get at deeply significant material; I explain that it is about establishing some sort of relationship. Then we spend time *exploring possibilities*. We raise sights; extend boundaries; challenge 'only one path'. Motorway thinking. Next I find myself *being a resource*: inputting ideas, offering books, whatever is needed. Then there is the important stage of *letting go*. It is unsatisfactory when they drift. Like Scottish country tunes, these relationships need to start and end clearly. It is important to review the journey with your travelling companion – this is where we thought we would go, this is what we have done, we are now at the parting of the ways.

There are no rules about whether mentor and mentee should be similar or different. They could be either, so long as you know which it is. I have a thing about values, though; I couldn't mentor someone whose values were very different from mine.

Mentoring for directors is most useful before there is a big problem. It is useful when they find they are giving out but not receiving; when you ask, 'Who do you get help from?' and they look lost or blank and can't think of anybody.

B4   Trish Longden, District Audit: professional career mentoring by Judy Weleminsky

Trish Longden is now the Director of People Development for District Audit – a full Board member. When she started this mentoring relationship she worked at Board level assisting the Chief Executive but was not a full Board member.

I see mentoring as a partnership with an agreed purpose in which the mentor supports the mentee through a significant life or work transition. It involves a formal commitment and framework but the approach, content and style need to be informal and tailored to the individual concerned.

I sought a mentor because I felt it could help me with specific work challenges and transitions I wanted to make. I discussed the competencies required with David Clutterbuck, who identified Judy Weleminsky as a potential mentor. We met and decided we could work together.

My expectations were largely optimistic, including access to broader experience, support, challenge and depth of analysis. My fears were that the relationship would not prove worthwhile so I would not find the time.

The range of issues we addressed included:

* influencing and forming strategic alliances
* communication
* the role of women on Boards – especially ones which are mostly male!
* detailed specific work issues.

We were able to reflect and explore together the issues that were challenging me at any particular time and consider how past approaches worked and were progressing. I did prepare for the meetings, but I always felt I should have done more.

The most valued skills and qualities that the mentor brought to the relationship were:

* understanding of and interest in relationships at work
* openness
* willingness to share her own experiences
* ability to keep focused and targeted
* determination to plug away at the issues.

I believe the influence in the relationship was exercised fairly equally on the quickly established basis of trust. We developed an open way of working. I felt that my mentor brought rigour and preparation to our sessions, which are not my strengths, while I brought enthusiasm and excitement.

The relationship ended formally when we had achieved our purpose. The problems were mostly making time – we were both very busy – but nonetheless we made it a priority and were flexible. Sometimes we strayed into personal areas voluntarily and with interest. I felt very positively about the relationship and expressed that to my mentor and to others when mentioning my mentoring relationship.

I felt there were four stages in our relationship:

1   We developed a shared understanding of issues.
2   Together we developed possible ways forward and I tried them out.
3   The ideas worked – which was critical to adding impetus to our relationship.
4   I achieved promotion to the Board – success!

I felt we had achieved the outcomes I wanted and this reinforced for me the value of mentoring. I now advocate it to others and I miss the time I enjoyed with my mentor. I have very warm feelings towards my mentor and I particularly valued the way she celebrated my success. There is nothing I would change about my mentor. I hope that she got pleasure from the relationship, not just its success but also personal growth from the discussions and some fun.

B5 Philip Lewer, City of Bradford Social Services: mentoring with heart

Philip Lewer is Assistant Director of Social Services for the City of Bradford Metropolitan District Council. He has a budget of £36 million and manages approximately 2800 staff, most of them women working part-time. He went to Bradford in 1977 and stays there because he loves it.

I have had three mentors. My first was a psychiatrist and medical director called Simon Baugh. He was a close colleague working in the NHS, and we spent time looking at what each of us do. We have carried on meeting roughly once every three months – not socially, but he takes an interest in my managerial growth, and I take an interest in him. He showed me that even if, in my thinking, I went all the way through 360° back to the direction I started from, it was worth it for the journey. He showed me that if you have both doubts and a lot of staff, then it is important to be clear about the decisions you have already made and about what is still open for negotiation.

We do not use the term mentoring – he calls and says, 'I could do with some of your quality time.' He has helped me to broaden my experience rather than go higher in my career; for example, he has encouraged me to do work in Hungary and Estonia. He helps me to concentrate on the things that I can change; we talk about the different approaches I can take to situations and to the teams I manage. He takes a massive interest in what I do and in me as an individual, and because he works in a related field he has an insight into the issues I face.

We both look at developing services for people with mental ill health. On one occasion when people were getting precious about alternate approaches to the work, Simon said, 'Why are we arguing about this? There's enough mental illness in Bradford for all of us!' I decided then that he was someone I could work with. We have used a whiteboard wiped clean to plan our services from scratch.

When a session goes well, we go to a Mexican restaurant together and have a toffee pudding as a treat.

A more recent mentor is Professor Hadley, who I met in 1987 and who has been my mentor since 1990. He was my professor when I did a Masters degree at Lancaster University. I left school with one 'O' Level, and he said I was a joy to teach because he could watch me grow, as I grappled with tasks like producing 8500 words of coherent argument. He warms to my enthusiasm.

I see him for a day twice a year in his house in Wales where he has lived since he retired. He also sends me books to read. He takes notes of our conversations and sometimes records them. He gives me a zest for learning, and faith and confidence in my own ability to learn. The thing that amazed me was his belief in me as a person. We first started meeting at a time of considerable stress for me – my father had just died and all my hair fell out. He has nurtured me.

When he was still at the university I would run a session for him on a Social Science course, so that was bartering a bit for what he did for me. I send him things I have written; he is encouraging me to write a book, though his way of writing and mine would be very different – my way is from the heart rather than from the head. That is the joy of the relationship – learning from difference. It is not a friendship – we don't meet apart from this.

These two mentors – Simon Baugh and Roger Hadley (six years down the line, and now he's retired, I can call him Roger) – have also ended up mentoring me on how I mentor others.

A third mentor is a woman social work team leader who works in another division of my department. She is of mixed race, and when I became a manager, Margaret helped me take a step back and look at race issues in a non-confrontational way. She suggests things to read and think about.

I speak to her over the phone once a week and see her perhaps once a month. On these occasions we sometimes have a drink together. The relationship is bordering upon friendship, in a way that the other two are not.

She was the first black woman I had come into contact with who didn't seem angry. She works in another part of my organization and gives me useful insights about how things are perceived. I see her as a mentor – I am not sure whether she sees it that way.

All these relationships are a very important way for me to create space. I work in a local government department that has got almost frantic – with more and more being asked of fewer and fewer people. What has helped is having people who have taken an interest, and given me confidence in trying new and different things.

I see my mentors as being totally different from me; I think other mentoring relationships have failed because I was not able to be explicit about what I was looking for. Relationships that have worked have started informally – I have been impelled to seek something by an awareness of my own lack of something. At the start I have had fears of exposing too much of myself and being vulnerable, but as the relationship gets more established these fears disappear.

Taking a wider view, a lot of it is to do with how you see yourself; being honest with yourself. I was told at school that I was no good; my first boss told me she didn't like the way I breathed. There are bits of myself that I don't like, but I know I can reduce these with my mentors! I have faced the prospect of thinking I was about to die. Life is an adventure and mentors help you to live it fully.

The mentoring I have had helps me to give back a bit to others. I am allocated as a mentor when people go on open learning courses. There are one or two of these who have used me because they think that I am in a position of power and I can help with their careers. What I have done is give them references.

One of the people I mentor currently is a lecturer who started work as one of the first Asian social workers in Bradford. We talk every six months or so. He sounds ideas off and thinks things through, and sends me things he has written. I see myself as a mentor to him, but I get things out of it too. It is nice to feel that someone values your opinion and I like to feel I am passing on things I've learned. As with Professor Hadley and me, it is good to see someone grow and to think you've made a small contribution to that.

There is one person who I mentored for a fixed two-year period while he did a course. That started on a fairly formal basis as I was allocated to him. We explored together how he could create space, to give him time to think. He worked it all out for himself. He could be more productive, at work and on the course, if he gave himself two or three hours each week to reflect. He also widened his experience by job shadowing – initially for a day with me, and then with people who he had difficulty with, seeing things from their point of view. He said he learned more from me than from any other aspect of his course.

There are a number of others, but let me tell you about one relationship that I am about to start. We have a joint unit run between Social Services and the Health Service. I have been asked to mentor the manager who runs the unit. I have agreed to see her for 12 sessions, and to explore the two cultures and to see how she can grow between the two organizations. We are doing this for the greater good of the people of Bradford. This is the first time someone from outside the Department has recommended someone to use me as a mentor, so I come with some credibility that I didn't know I had.

B6   Dan Sequerra, Executive Director, Kirklees Metropolitan Council: a mentoring champion

Dan Sequerra is one of a small team of directors at the pinnacle of Kirklees Metropolitan Council, a local authority with a strong reputation for innovative methods of delivering quality services.

I first came across mentoring in 1985 when I was Director of Employment at Sheffield Council. I see it as 'looking out for people and encouraging them'. We were strongly interested in the development of all staff – including junior people. I was impressed by the amount of talent we released there. The first programme was for 25 women, and many now have reached senior positions. The person who ran the programme went from a junior management job to become a Chief Officer in another authority. The programme was about recognizing, encouraging and developing the potential that was there.

Mentoring is best done relatively informally, because once it is formalized it gets intimidating. However, we have introduced formal mentoring with a management training initiative for junior and middle managers called the Kirklees Management Certificate, which we co-deliver with Sheffield Hallam University. It was felt that a mentoring component needed to be introduced because it could not be assumed that the delegates on the course would be informally mentored. It was felt that someone other than their supervisors should assist them, even though we did encourage the managers to become involved in the process. These managers later expanded into contributing as mentors to other programmes, enlarging our pool.

Now, we integrate mentoring fully into all our management development schemes. We have kept enough informality to deal with it as a personal process with choice for the mentee. Having a register of mentors is useful, then mentees can choose from this list.

You cannot predict all the outcomes of personal development and you cannot put boundaries on how people develop. It is about helping people to anticipate their own development needs and think about where they might be in 3–5 years' time. If your model of mentoring is about organization development, then you need development both for careers and within the job. Mentoring and development is not just for career-driven successful individuals; however, there is a transactional benefit in creating learning opportunities from the contacts that senior management mentors have. In an open appointment environment, it is legitimate for people to maximize their personal capital in competing for jobs internally.

In my view, a mentor is a good listener: someone who is able to grasp the development path that people are taking, and to assist with that. They can get some understanding of where people are trying to get to, and help them when they don't know where they want to go. A mentor can give impartial advice and practical help. A lot of it is about networking – often a mentor knows someone who can help and can put people in touch with others. I am mentoring a senior manager who meets me informally. He is looking for a career move so he wants to talk with someone about opportunities. For senior management, mentoring outside of our direct line of responsibility keeps us in touch with things. Mentors are another ear and sometimes (though not often) a shoulder to cry on. Any good manager should be doing some mentoring as part of their management role. I see it as the most important part of my job.

People should be free to choose their mentors. If they are particularly empathetic with their manager then that is fine. I would be very disappointed if the eight heads of service that report to me did not feel mentored in some sense – either formally or informally. Some, who are doing the top management programme with the Local Government Management Board, have also found their own; some have taken on mentors lower down the organization. I have done this myself, with a senior training person, who is now a Chief Officer in another authority. I was a key customer of hers for her training and development services, but we handled these roles without any problems.

We have always tried to provide mentors internally. In extreme cases we might pay for an external mentor, but that is very expensive. If mentoring is to be developed on any scale, there have to be internal processes at work. There are great benefits to the organization from this.

I have not been formally mentored, but I have taken people as mentors and used them as such virtually throughout through my career. Rob Hughes, who was Chief Executive here, has been a kindred spirit, and I have bounced things off him. The other person that I learned from was John Evans, who was an Executive Director here. He was very different from me. We found that we were doing lots of things together, and I was interested in the way he did things differently. I learned a lot from him.

B7   David Wilson, Director of Finance, NHS Trust: a personal account by Richard Hale and Jonathon Harding, IMC Consulting

Here we explore the experiences of a Finance Director from a British National Health Service Trust, who reflects on the value of his experience as a mentee. The name of the mentee has been changed to preserve anonymity. However, any quotations are taken directly from a transcript of the interview with him.

David has had a mentoring relationship for three years. One of the triggers for his embarking on this formal mentoring relationship was a discussion with his Director of Personnel about his development needs. Furthermore, he had a personal belief that there would be some value in mentoring. This was his first personal experience of mentoring and he hoped that it would provide an opportunity to explore immediate issues as well as longer-term development needs with somebody neutral, who was based outside his organization.

The mentor eventually identified was a Chief Executive from another NHS Trust. David feels that both parties have benefited, and he says that from time to time they have talked about how they have ended up mentoring each other. Some of the things he wanted to discuss as mentee were in fact helpful for the mentor too.

One of the major challenges in establishing a mentoring relationship is how the two parties are matched up. There is a range of possibilities:

- Unassigned – naturally evolving: Mutual selection
- Brokering of relationship by a
  third party: Range of options considered
- Suggestion by a third party: Limited choice for mentor/mentee
- Assigned by a third party: No mentor or mentee choice

David's experience of matching was that 'selecting the partner was quite interesting. It was based on advice from a third party. I suppose that on reflection I would do more screening or checking, now I know more about mentoring. I know it is easy to say afterwards, but I had never had a mentor, so I took advice from other people when choosing one.'

David sees the key issues in selecting a mentor as the need to find someone who you can get along with and, at the same time, who you can hold in respect. David noted that his own style is very different from that of his mentor:

> We're probably chalk and cheese, and that reflects the teams we work in. I work in a very people-oriented team. He works in an organization that places a lot of value on systems, processes and paper. It is an interesting tension. When I talk about the way we do things here, how we achieve results, he suggests a totally different perspective – a view that forces me to think and evaluate why I am doing and saying things in my current way. There is a tension, but both of us know that neither has the complete answer. It's not that sort of relationship. I'm not asking the 'what' and 'how' questions expecting direct answers. It's more about mutual exploration and suspending judgement. We do not set out to resolve our problems and the problems of the Health Service. We usually consider how we can handle situations more effectively. It comes back to the issue about tensions, about seeing things from different perspectives.

David describes being able to discuss his long-term development as a major benefit of the relationship:

> The longer it goes on, the more we tend to focus on structuring meetings around delivery of objectives and particular issues. The relationship is getting more focused as we get to understand each other. For me, one of the issues we have always dwelt on, which has been of real benefit, has been my long-term career development. This is an issue I don't always get into in my own organization. Within the management team we are not inclined to talk about issues such as when and why I might want to leave. In the mentoring relationship, we have talked about what I am doing now and where I want to be. The neutrality of the mentoring relationship allows these discussions. My mentor really keeps probing on this issue of career development. He has an eye for the long term, and he has my interests at heart. I find this useful – it's easy to know whether you're happy or not in a role, but who else could keep an eye on my long-term development? That for me has been the key benefit of my mentoring relationship.

David emphasized that he also challenged his mentor about his views on the qualities of an effective Chief Executive. He noted that this had been quite difficult for his mentor, but feels that, as an outsider, he has been able to get beneath the Chief Executive badge to reach the Chief Executive person.

The confidentiality of the relationship was seen as critical to success.

> There is something valuable about confidentiality. It's an opportunity to explore, to make mistakes and suggest stupid approaches, to be a bit creative or off the wall, without feeling

that you are being judged. There is the sounding board role. For example, I went on a Learning Set Programme. When I came back we discussed some of the positives and negatives of the experience in terms of my learning: feedback on how I look at problems, on what I was like, how I react. Indeed, there was some interesting information about my intolerance. Having a mentor helped me explore and confirm this feedback. This helped me to incorporate the ideas into everyday practice. My mentor assisted in this process by asking questions that helped me to understand, for example, that it is legitimate to be intolerant at times. One of the things I have learned through my mentor is about different behaviours for different situations. That simple view has been quite interesting for me. It has helped me make a transition from a traditional, functional, technical background, to that of a leader of a function that is integrated into an organization. One other specific thing that has been very useful is the issue of 'doctors in management' and how to manage doctors. This is useful for me to explore, because this is my first job working with doctors.

David also noted that in his mentoring meetings he was able to talk confidentially about lifestyle and the tensions between personal and work life. He said that this worked both ways, with his mentor also talking about his own feelings about this.

David takes a proactive approach to setting up meetings. He considers, ahead of the meeting, the issues for discussion. The meetings are usually in an informal setting, often over a meal. This combination of informality with defined objectives has been seen to work well.

David expressed the view that a lot of one's learning takes place in the work environment, and that this is probably the greatest source of learning. The mentoring role, says David, is about providing the stimulus for reflection and helping to construct the links and identify the principles associated with real life experiences.

David's relationship has been through a number of stages, and he has appraised it at a time when it was possible that it might come to an end. 'We had a discussion about three months ago about whether it should finish. Initially, we both thought it should. I think I may have changed my view, so we are meeting up to talk about that. I can see that I need a mentor now more than at any time in the last 20 years. Like all these things, when you are faced with something coming to an end, you start to explore its value more carefully.'

Points emerging from David's experience as a mentee are:

- An external mentor can provide a powerful support mechanism for senior managers.

- Confidentiality in the relationship is crucial.
- Contrasts in style may provide a strength and synergy in the relationship.
- A balance between structure and purpose on the one hand, and informality on the other, works well.
- The mentee needs to be the driving force in the relationship.
- Mentoring is a 'whole-life' process, and it can be helpful to discuss development in a holistic way.
- Potentially, the mentor stands to gain as much as the mentee from a successful relationship.
- Reappraisal of the relationship at intervals is important and may focus minds on the benefits.

C1 Sir Christopher Ball, Chancellor of Derby University, Chairman, Campaign for Learning

Sir Christopher is a portfolio worker with a passion for learning and development – his own and others'. After ten years as Warden of Keble College, Oxford, he set out to develop the Royal Society of Arts Lifelong Learning project.

I encountered my mentor, Barry Oxtoby, the Chief Executive of the Rover Learning Business, at a conference where we were both speaking. I was excited by what I heard from Barry about the Rover process using Personal Learning Plans. So I asked Barry in public to be my mentor. That way, he had no choice but to accept.

I see mentoring being used in two senses: the first is an adult helping another adult work on a Personal Learning Plan; this is different from a more interventionist relationship where someone with expertise helps another person, who may be another adult or a young person. My relationship with Barry is of the first kind. It is informal, with no rules, and a very happy one.

He supports me in working with my Personal Learning Plan, and the relationship is driven from the learner's side. Barry is relatively passive, but not completely. The Learning Plan asks me some questions: 'What do I want to be in five years time?', 'What learning do I have to do to achieve that?' I make a learning inventory of what I have done before – which is very exciting because you find how brilliant you are! What is *really* exciting is that this happens to *everybody* who makes a learning plan.

I find it valuable to have a mentor to challenge, to prompt and to say, 'Well done.' When he saw my first plan three years ago Barry asked, 'What about your voluntary work?' I wasn't clear that this counted, but he said, 'Put it in and let's look at it.' When I completed my first plan, I discovered that I was a terrible boaster – I had put all kinds of things in because they looked good. This was pointless, because only Barry and my wife see it. So nowadays I stay much more focused.

I decided to review my plan once a year and then have a major discussion with Barry. His 'big question' is, 'What did you learn from that, Christopher?' I sometimes joke in speeches that, based on my experience of Barry, asking this question is all you need to do to be a mentor. The question is very useful whether you succeed or fail.

If I have extra things I want to learn during the year, I just add them. A lot of learning happens anyway, even though it is not expected. I tell Barry about these changes. He rings me from time to time, and we meet occasionally between the yearly reviews of the PLP.

When he telephones me he is often challenging. Recently he called and asked whether I had been on the time management course I planned to attend. When I said, 'No,' he replied, 'I thought not; I gather you spoke too long at a conference last week.' So I do get a feeling that he is willing to check me out and assess progress.

I sometimes go back through the PLP process, like pulling it up by the roots to see if it's growing. I then send the changes to Barry. He suggests I throw things away too easily; sometimes I think he would like me to be steadier.

Currently I am getting interested in the problem of what a man is to do with his life between 60 and 80 (I am 62). Barry asks me, 'What do you *want* to do?' In the earlier stages of my life I knew what was expected of me, but now it is not clear. It helps to have a mentor.

I have recently taken on some voluntary work, which has provided me with some challenging training in counselling, and another mentor. Richard follows what I call the 'Ninja Principle': 'Never Interfere; Never Judge or Advise'. He is more passive than Barry, and when we meet his question is no more than, 'How are you getting on then?'

I have a third mentor, Charles Handy, and ten years ago he encouraged me to lead the portfolio life. He would probably be surprised that I call him a mentor, as we meet primarily on a family friendship basis – but we explore our different models of the portfolio life. We add things to each other's experience – but he is the senior partner.

Mentors seldom prompt you to do something specific. I don't think you can do the job unless you listen very well. My wife said to Barry that she thought his mentoring role was impossible, 'because Christopher is unteachable'.

However, I have learned a lot from being with each of my mentors. Each of them has come to have an intimate knowledge of me as part of the relationship. You start by expecting it to be about the job, and then it becomes about personal matters and those near and dear to you.

I currently have two mentees – a businessman who runs a manufacturing company and a senior executive at a Training and Enterprise Council. In each case I was tremendously flattered to be asked.

One is going very slowly indeed. His work and his circumstances get in the way. I have telephoned him a number of times and we have met on one or two occasions. Last time he set himself a lot of tasks, and he tells me he is so busy he hasn't done them. I say, 'Yes, it's tough, a matter of priorities.' So although I remind him, it is up to him to drive the process.

The other person is going much further and faster. He has read all the books and is extremely well organized – much more than I am in my sessions with Barry. His plan is much more comprehensive and elaborate than mine, with separate sections for himself as a person, family, community and work. He turns up to our sessions fully organized, and my role is just to ask him, 'Why did that happen?' I help him see recurring patterns. One is that he tries to involve others in his plans and they often resist – he is aiming to make them what he wants them to be. So that leads us into exploring personal relationships. It is a privilege to be sitting on the edge of this, wondering when it is appropriate to challenge.

So even if we adhere to the Ninja Principle, in practice, as mentors, we inevitably lead people towards certain issues. There is a balance between never interfering, judging or advising and the fact that any conversation with a lot of listening leads the other person to new thoughts and plans.

I think that everyone in the country ought to have a Personal Learning Plan. It has to be written down to provide a challenge. It is *wise* to have a mentor to support it.

C2 Dorothy Newton, RIBA: a voluntary sector director by Judy Weleminsky

Dorothy Newton was Acting Director of the Federation of Independent Advice Centres. She is now Librarian Consultant for the Royal Institute of British Architecture.

I understand mentoring as a form of counselling, within the context of the relationship with the organization. It provides support, safe listening and is particularly important for isolated Chief Executives. It is both formal and informal. Perhaps it is counselling in the old-fashioned sense.

I sought a mentor because I felt isolated from my former colleagues as a result of my promotion to Acting Director. My mentor found me! She heard me voicing concerns on a training course and took up the issues with me in a coffee break.

My trustees were positive about the idea of a mentor, recognizing that I needed support, which they were not able to provide. They suggested two other mentors but they were unsuitable because they were too close to the organization and also too close to me. I wanted someone who could bring a dispassionate point of view and who had wider senior experience of the sector I worked in. The others were both male and I valued the fact that Judy was female, helping to increase my confidence about women working at this level.

I had some fears about the relationship – that it would expose my lack of experience and sophistication. In reality we concentrated much more on practical issues involved in managing my situation and containing the conflicting pressures. Because of the way our relationship started and the emphatic nature of my mentor, I felt it was fruitful very quickly. I found the mentor helped me to reflect. She often challenged and gave advice, and I saw her as a role model. In the long term, I feel the self-knowledge and opportunity for reflection were particularly helpful. It helped me to keep my sanity, sense of perspective and self-confidence during a very stressful period.

I usually prepared for the meetings by making lists. Usually one item was top – also usually something would emerge. The gap between sessions acted as a pressure cooker.

My mentor's experience of similar situations, combined with her empathy, communication skills and ability to promote thinking, were particularly useful qualities and skills. The similarities and dissimilarities between us were both helpful and sometimes a barrier in taking forward our thinking.

The formal relationship ended when my position as Acting Director came to an end. The timing of this was quite difficult. It would have been helpful if it could have been longer term – less 'first aid'. I would also have liked more frequent sessions.

Overall I feel the outcome from the mentoring relationship has been that I am more aware of the role of self in the work situation – though not necessarily an improved ability to deal with it appropriately. I am applying aspects that I learned from the mentoring relationship to other work situations and relationships.

The lessons for executive and director mentoring

In Part 3 we offer the lessons that we have learned from our research in producing this book. Much of what we say here is derived from the wisdom and reflection of the people we have interviewed and the insight of our collaborators.

We, as authors, have identified the crucial issues in executive mentoring, and we take full responsibility for this choice. However, we were hugely helped in coming to a view about the issues by a number of directors who feature in one capacity or another in Part 2 of this book.

The process that we used in eliciting the views of these directors was as follows. We prepared a range of cases from Part 2 and invited three directors to examine them. Of these three, one was chairman of a private sector British company, one a senior director of a vibrant public sector organization, and one a director of a European institution. The directors and the authors spent some time reading the cases, choosing the ones to focus upon on the basis of their interests. They then discussed the cases that they had read and drew the others' attention to the matters that engaged them. From this discussion a range of issues started to emerge and points were made and debated. We recorded these points and used them as a basis for the agenda when writing this part of the book.

The issues

The broad issues that emerged as crucial for executive and director mentoring were grouped as follows:

1   Organization issues
2   Mentee role and behaviour
3   Mentor role and behaviour
4   Relationship issues.

With the help of our director advisors we identified a series of topics within these issues, which are addressed in the remainder of this book.

Organization issues

Mentoring does not take place in a vacuum. Even if the executive or director pays for it themselves and does not tell anyone in their organization that it is happening, it will have effects which will impact on others and the organization. As we said in Part 1, mentoring is a powerful organizational intervention. It speaks to the needs of very senior managers, because it helps them to address their own pressing issues, which are often closely related to the organizational issues that we discuss below:

- Contributing to change management
- CEO support
- Internal vs. external mentors
- For whom? Universal or focused
- Ownership of mentoring
- Global management issues.

Contributing to change management

The directors we spoke with said it was important to consider organizational impacts of executive mentoring as well as the individual effects. Some of the points they made were:

- Mentoring is crucial to organizational development.
- Executive mentors need an underlying model that links director development to organizational development.
- One way that this can be achieved is by linking mentoring to established organization growth models such as the balanced scorecard, organizational transformation or the European Foundation for Quality management framework. These models can be used to throw light on the issues that need to be addressed in the mentoring relationship.

In one major retail organization where we are advising on mentoring and coaching, the Board has approved a set of leadership characteristics. Top management one-to-one executive coaching is designed to help directors to manifest these characteristics in their work. This integrated approach links the individual coaching of executives to the change programme of the organization. It is less individually tailored than the rather anarchic one-to-one mentoring typical of many major organizations. Scheme organizers will need to decide whether to focus their approach to executive mentoring upon integration with organization goals or customization to individuals' needs.

CEO support

Whether mentoring is focused on the individual or on the broader needs of the organization, it needs support from the very top. Carl Eric Gestberg's case of ABB (A5), Nick Holley at Lex (A7) and Trude Stolpe at Axel Johnsson (A11) are examples of this from the private sector. A public sector example is Dan Sequerra at Kirklees (B6). In all the cases with good CEO support, it was manifested not just in words, but also in the CEO offering to be a mentor personally. In many cases where outside mentors were used, the CEO was the first to become a mentee. Nick Holley illustrates these themes when he says:

> It has been critical to have active involvement from the top. Our Chief Executive has stated that management development is one of his three key drivers and a strategic core competence for Lex. The top team value mentoring as a core part of this commitment. He and all the Management Board have been actively involved as mentors. They were the first people to use the process. They have seen the benefits for themselves, giving credibility to the idea and providing role models.

This is a challenge for CEOs to take up and for their advisors to put to them.

Internal vs. external mentors

Discussion of the CEO's role brings us on to the issue of whether to use internal or external mentors for the top management team. There are cost considerations, as Dan Sequerra (B6) says:

> We have always tried to provide mentors internally. In extreme cases we might pay for an external mentor, but that is very expensive. If mentoring is to be developed on any scale, there have to be internal processes at work. There are great benefits to the organization from this.

Another argument for internal mentors is that they can perpetuate a successful culture. If this is one of the purposes of executive mentoring, then clearly it is sensible to use internal mentors. Carl Eric Gestberg at ABB (A5) illustrates this:

> ABB Sweden has 130 companies, so they could easily find a mentor outside their own company. They could also go outside ABB, if they wanted, but that is very rare.

A similar point is made by Trude Stolpe (A11):

> We decided that mentoring could be very useful in increasing understanding between levels in the organization and between generations . . . The key objectives [included] perpetuate the corporate culture.

On the other hand, David Wilson, a Finance Director in an NHS Trust (B7) says:

> For me, one of the issues we have always dwelt on, which has been of real benefit, has been my long-term career development.

> This is an issue I don't always get into in my own organization.
> Within the management team we are not inclined to talk about
> issues such as when and why I might want to leave. In the
> mentoring relationship, we have talked about what I am doing
> now and where I want to be. The neutrality of the mentoring
> relationship allows these discussions.

As well as this concern about confidentiality, another case for external mentors is that the talent or the perspective required may not be available internally. As Kees Zandvliet (A13) says:

> It would be preferable if we could do this with each other inside
> the company, but I do question the possibilities of this. A mentor
> from outside probably has an easier, less emotional starting point.

So, a key issue seems to be: 'Do we want executive and director mentoring to perpetuate an effective existing culture or to change an unsatisfactory one?' If the former, go for internal mentors. If the latter, then external ones may be the only source of a new direction.

For whom? Universal or focused

Another factor which influences whether internal or external mentors are used is the question of who the mentoring is for. On the one hand there are the universalists who argue that mentoring should be accessible for everyone within the a particular category of employee. Carl Eric Gestberg of ABB (A5) is typical of these:

> For ABB, mentoring is a continuous process. In 1991, we had
> 150 women involved in mentoring relationships; in 1992 there
> were 250. In 1998, we had 3000 people involved – both men
> and women.

Dan Sequerra (B6) from the public sector is another advocate of universalism:

> We were strongly interested in the development of all staff –
> including junior people. I was impressed by the amount of talent
> we released there ... If your model of mentoring is about
> organization development, then you need development both for
> careers and within the job. Mentoring and development is not
> just for career-driven successful individuals ...

In the voluntary sector, Sir Christopher Ball (C1) is an arch-universalist:

> I think that everyone in the country ought to have a Personal
> Learning Plan. It has to be written down to provide a challenge.
> It is *wise* to have a mentor to support it.

On the other hand there are those cases where mentoring is seen as being focused on the members of the executive cadre most valued by those making decisions about careers and succession. Nick Holley at Lex (A7) says:

> In our succession processes we have identified a number of
> people at executive level that we feel are critical to our future.
> In each case we have allocated to them a member of the
> executive team (including the Chairman and Chief Executive) as
> a mentor.

Similarly, Trude Stolpe at Axel Johnsson (A11) says:

> Then we asked the CEO of each division to propose a number
> of mentees – high flyers typically in their mid-30s.

This is another decision that scheme organizers and sponsors will need to make – is mentoring for senior people in the organization designed to make a change for everybody or does it have a focus on fast-track careers and succession?

Ownership of mentoring

Paradoxically, it is an HR Director who talks tough about mentoring not being owned by HR. Nick Holley (A7) says of Lex's scheme:

> As a result of our beginning the process and the successes that
> have happened, mentoring relationships are springing up all over
> Lex. In many cases, we have no idea that it is happening. Shock
> horror – we aren't in control! Perhaps that is the reason for
> success . . . Success has not come from a big central push. We
> have provided the initial idea but people have adopted it, seen
> value in it and run with it. Ownership in the business, not at the
> centre, is everything.

He also makes the point that we should not follow what his company has done – what is good for Lex may not be right in our circumstances. However, his experience provides a useful challenge for committed centralizers.

Global management issues

We have written earlier (Megginson and Clutterbuck, 1995, pp. 15–16) about the distinction between American and European mentoring. We see the US variety as emphasizing career and sponsorship issues while the European version tends to emphasize learning and personal change. This was reinforced for one of the authors recently in a discussion with a group of directors from a number of companies. Several of the directors had talked about a helping relationship which they had valued, and in each case the outcomes had been expressed in terms of insights, awareness, confidence, breadth of perspective. Then a man talked of his relationship, which had involved promoting his career and sponsorship. We were able to risk the prediction that the company had been American – it was, archetypally perhaps, Avon Cosmetics.

In this book, the case of Allen Yurko of Siebe (A12) also follows a characteristic American pattern. His candid account of his rise and rise through a string of American companies includes phrases such as, 'He was the major proponent for me to become . . .', '. . . he assigned me the job of . . .' and 'That was a direct attempt to get me operating responsibility . . .'

We were interested to see if we could identify differences between European countries in their approach to mentoring. We obtained relatively little hard and fast data, but from what we were able to garner the following tentative conclusions could be drawn.

France. The formality of French executive life makes mentoring difficult to acknowledge and difficult to practise. Liz Borredon's respondent (A2) was open and curious, and was both mentee and mentor. However, he acknowledged that he was sharply atypical of his peers and both he and Liz Borredon recognize the difficulty in French culture for senior managers of seeking and using personal help.

Holland. The case studies written by Lida Beers (A10) and by Nina Lazeron (A13) both emphasize the way that informal relaxed attitudes and relationships are valued in the Netherlands. It is not surprising that the one case of peer mentoring in the book is Lida Beers' account of four senior Dutch executives. Nina Lazeron's case of Kees Zandvliet in Heineken also has characteristic informal features – the mix of personal and professional, the network of contacts to find the right person, the growing from one-way to two-way help and respect. Perhaps there is a characteristic Dutch model emerging from these stories.

Sweden. Trude Stolpe's evaluation of executive mentoring in Axel Johnsson (A11), and Carl Eric Gestberg's account of ABB (A5), have characteristics we have found in other Swedish mentoring efforts known to us, including Swedish Nestlé (reported in Megginson and Clutterbuck, 1995), and both Telia and SAS (Megginson and Clutterbuck, 1998). Swedish mentoring seems to have strong sponsorship from a powerful HR function, endorsed by the CEO of the corporation who also 'walks the talk' by being involved as a mentor. The arrangements for the mentoring seem to be well researched and planned and to involve all members of a particular category of employee. Goals seem to be egalitarian (better understanding between levels; exchange of knowledge and experience; all the responsibility on the mentee to find the help they need) and conservative (perpetuate the corporate culture; very rare to go outside the company for a mentor).

Britain. What do these examples tell us about the approach to executive mentoring in Britain? With many more cases from Britain in the book, the diversity (which of course will be there in every country) shows through. Nonetheless, the contrast with the other countries indicates some features which are relatively widespread in Britain.

The goals of British mentoring are most frequently around insight, learning and personal support in dealing with challenges and crises. The style of relationship seems to be affected by the way in which people who become mentors often have a charismatic personal style and a clear vision of how to be and how to develop. This means that the mentors tend to share their insights and also challenge the mentee. In the sectors where we have the most information about senior executive mentoring (including information systems, banks and retail), executive mentoring is often ad hoc. There is a multiplicity of suppliers, or if there is one official supplier then some executives will go elsewhere and fund the mentoring from their line budget or out of their own pocket.

Table 3.1 summarizes these comparisons. It challenges us to explore whether our approach to mentoring is shaped by our national culture and whether we might not learn something from the approach of mentors elsewhere that would be relevant in our particular circumstances. More specifically it raises some pertinent questions for those mentoring across national boundaries, such as:

- Does my partner have the same expectations about the relationship as I do?
- How can we address our national differences in expectations?
- What would a resolution of these differences be like?

Mentee role and behaviour

We have put this section on the role of the mentee before the one on the role of the mentor for two reasons. First, it symbolizes that the mentee comes first. Second, and more specifically, we must understand the

Table 3.1   Comparison of characteristic approaches to executive mentoring by country

Country	Goals	Style of relationship	Features of schemes
US	Sponsorship Promoting career	Paternalistic	Senior director taking up cause of younger high flyer
France	Insight Analysis of life purpose	Commitment to sharing values	Scheme created outside companies
Netherlands	Mutual support Learning Networking	Informal Egalitarian Peer mentoring Universal Egalitarian	Recognizing benefits for mentor and mentee Personal and professional
Sweden	Perpetuate culture	Share understanding Exchange knowledge	Strong sponsorship from HR and CEO Well researched and planned Involves all in category targeted
Britain	Insight Learning Support	Individualistic Charismatic mentor shares insight and challenges mentee	Ad hoc Diversity of opportunities

characteristics and needs of the mentee in order to find out what the mentor needs to do and know. Start with the mentee's dream, as Richard Caruso, the Chairman, President and CEO of Integra Lifesciences Corporation, said at the 1996 European Mentoring Conference (Caruso, 1996). In this section we address the following points:

- Help with director role
- Isolation at the top
- 'Won't be told'
- Evolution of mentoring need and role modelling
- Outcomes for mentees.

Help with director role

There is a crucial transition in moving from being a senior manager responsible for a function and being a director with a responsibility for overseeing the entire organization and for corporate governance. Bob Garratt (1996) suggests that directors need to develop a broader mindset to deal with the uncertainties of policy formulation, strategic thinking and accountability. Mentors can greatly assist with this transition. Colin Palmer (A8a) says:

> Because I have been there, I talk them through such issues as professional indemnity exposure, registering trade names, preparing for due diligence searches, which require specific advice.

Others, such as Julia Essex (B1b), get help with this role from elsewhere. However, executives who have newly become directors will be on a very steep learning curve and this is an exceptionally important time to have a mentor – often of the elder statesperson variety described in Part 1. If new directors are unaware of the difference between managing and directing then it is crucial that they have help of this kind.

Isolation at the top

We see isolation at the top of organizations as being due to a number of factors, which we summarize in Figure 3.1 – the trust barrier.

As can be seen in the figure, we suggest that there are a series of parallel processes engaged in by both directors and others in the organization. This mutual stand-off is held in place by a shared sense of hopelessness, embodied in the phrase, 'They will never change', which

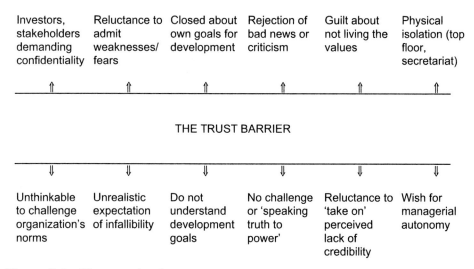

Investors, stakeholders demanding confidentiality	Reluctance to admit weaknesses/ fears	Closed about own goals for development	Rejection of bad news or criticism	Guilt about not living the values	Physical isolation (top floor, secretariat)
⇑	⇑	⇑	⇑	⇑	⇑

THE TRUST BARRIER

⇓	⇓	⇓	⇓	⇓	⇓
Unthinkable to challenge organization's norms	Unrealistic expectation of infallibility	Do not understand development goals	No challenge or 'speaking truth to power'	Reluctance to 'take on' perceived lack of credibility	Wish for managerial autonomy

Figure 3.1 The trust barrier

can be widely heard on both sides of the barrier. Of course, people in the best organizations dismantle the barriers, but it is not an easy task. Argyris (1993) suggests that it is not only that so much in organizations is unsayable. There is also the added problem that the fact that these things are unsayable cannot be acknowledged.

Mentors, especially external ones, can be helpful in exposing these degenerative barriers for directors. Sir Christopher Ball (C1) expresses this very clearly at a personal level:

> My wife said to Barry that she thought his mentoring role was impossible, 'because Christopher is unteachable'.
>
> However, I have learned a lot from being with each of my mentors. Each of them has come to have an intimate knowledge of me as part of the relationship. You start by expecting it to be about the job, and then it becomes about personal matters and those near and dear to you.

Having someone who is willing to stand up to you and challenge you is one of the major motives directors and executives have for taking on a mentor.

'Won't be told'

Dinah Bennett and Christina Hartshorn (A1) in their account of mentoring owner-managers say:

> It must be noted here that the learning in these cases is that of 'self-learning' and not being told what to do. Typical entrepreneurial owner-managers learn by doing, by learning from their mistakes. They perceive being advised or being told what to do as a threat to their autonomy. Hence, mentoring owner managers and those aspiring to run their own businesses brings with it unique problems and opportunities!

Entrepreneurs especially often exhibit the 'won't be told' syndrome, and this tends to reinforce the trust barrier, discussed above. However, all directors and executives are likely to display this characteristic to some extent. It is a strong personal challenge for such people to commit to learning with others, and there is a corresponding challenge for mentors to make sure that their help is confronting enough, without attempting to tell or to create dependency.

Evolution of mentoring need and role modelling

Many of our respondents have had a series of mentors over their careers. Allen Yurko (A12) is a good example. Directors who have been skilled multiple mentees know what issues to address at each stage of their development and find the person who can help them deal with that.

A particular example of evolution is where the mentee selects the mentor as a role model. We see this position as being only temporary,

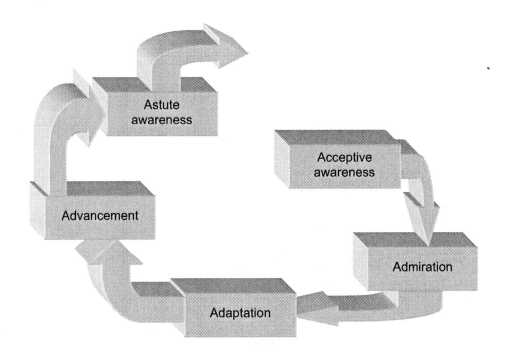

Figure 3.2 Model of mentoring role modelling

and we follow a schematic evolution of the path of a role modeller (see Figure 3.2), which mentees and mentors alike can use to be aware of the dynamics of this kind of relationship.

The stages are described in Table 3.2, with their features and an indication of what the mentee needs to do to move on within the relationship.

Role modelling has overtones of dependency, and while it can play an important part in mentoring relationships, it should be seen as a temporary phase.

Outcomes for mentees
Executive mentees can focus their effort in the mentoring relationship if they are clear about what type of outcome the wish to achieve from it.

Table 3.2   A model of role modelling in mentoring relationships

Stage	Features	To move on
Acceptive awareness	Based on reputation, observation from a distance; recognizing role model as source of learning	Seeking out the mentor or being sought out
Admiration	Development of regard based on the role model's values, impact and (sometimes) interest in mentee	Dissatisfaction with aspects of oneself, which the mentor appears to have mastered
Adaptation	Conscious and unconscious process of change to adopt role model's behaviour, ways of thinking, values	Tune in to the mentor's behaviours, ideas, strategies, motives; commit to personal change
Advancement	Integrate mentor's mental models with one's own; practise new behaviour and observe results	Step back and look at the mentor more critically
Astute awareness	Mature evaluation of the role model – warts and all; re-assert and also develop own values and mental models	Seek new sources of learning/role models; become more selective in distinguishing what to accept/reject

An analysis of Part 2 yielded over 50 separate statements of mentee outcome. These have been classified and listed below:

Business development

- brainstorming ideas about getting business
- move the business forward
- move the whole organization forward
- practical ideas and connections in the line of work.

Life purpose

- clarity of vision, clarity of direction
- clear sense of being valued

- find the work I want
- gain self-belief, continuously to raise horizons
- give back a bit to others
- live life fully
- loving learning and loving me for who I am
- make very significant choices in my life
- more effective in business creation and growth
- the sense of my life
- who I am, and what my place is, what I am here for.

Focus

- face up to tough decisions
- keep focused on the critical issues
- keep focused on the key issues
- look clearly at an issue without deviation.

Personal life/lifestyle/balance

- addressed lifestyle, balance in life
- progress in my relationship with my children
- resolve tensions between personal and work life.

Development plan/career plan

- a development plan which is actively supported
- able to discuss long-term career development
- dialogue about career
- working on Personal Learning Plan.

Career development/promotion/rewards

- a job that is stretching
- achieve a good career path
- achieved promotion to the Board
- become the youngest in a certain role
- focus on the future role and abilities
- found a new job
- made impressive careers
- widened experience by job shadowing
- a substantial bonus for taking on additional responsibility
- appropriate reward and recognition.

Self-awareness

- better self-knowledge and awareness
- more aware of the role of self in the work situation.

Breadth of insight

- better understanding between levels
- exchange of knowledge and experience
- insights into how things are perceived by others
- learn the stories that are told
- look at race issues in a non-confrontational way
- recognize how one acts and make conscious choices
- seeing the view from another pair of eyes to change practice
- wise about living in another culture, about marriage, life and how to do things.

Stress management

- help through a particularly bad patch with boss
- keep sanity, sense of perspective and self-confidence during stressful period
- personal coping mechanisms
- use unwelcome change as an opportunity to make choices.

Change behaviour or style

- challenged personal behaviour and commitment
- concentrate on the things that I can change
- express my concerns in a positive way
- helped to reflect
- reflecting on my own management style
- thinking through complex issues, especially about people
- to be the very best Chairman I could be
- zest for learning; faith and confidence in ability to learn.

Mentees can use the titles in the list above as a checklist for considering which area they would like to focus upon. They can use the items under each title as heartening examples of the kind of outcome that they might strive for.

Mentor role and behaviour

Our review of the mentor's role and behaviour takes place starting from the experience and the issues of the mentee, which we have discussed in the previous section. However, there are many issues which are the principal concern of the mentor; the ones we discuss here are:

- Qualities and role of mentors
- Preparation vs. planning
- Having a process

- Challenge and confrontation
- Crisis mentoring
- Supervision
- What's in it for me (WIIFM)?
- Pay and rewards.

Qualities and role of mentors

Our case studies illustrate a huge range of qualities. Some of the qualities highlighted by the directors were:

- Experience outside the organization
- Good questions
- Role modelling
- Credibility
- Good listener
- Patience
- Networking
- Helping the mentee become themselves
- Two-way insight sharing
- Balancing process and content
- Helping, enabling, supporting
- Helping to manage knowledge
- Being dependable.

This simple checklist is a good one for executives considering seeking a mentor to use in checking out their prospective candidates.

Another way of analysing what mentors do is to describe the roles they play. Liz Borredon's *accompagnateur* (A2) identifies four sorts of role mentors can play:

- Spiritual
- Relational
- Professional
- Technical.

Mentoring often gets to the edge of *spiritual* issues when it addresses life purpose. Our survey of outcomes for mentees in Part 2 indicates that this happens quite often in mentoring relationships. A smaller number of cases address spiritual issues directly (notably the *accompagnateur* (A2), Richard Field (A4) and Dame Rennie Fritchie (B3).

Relational matters came up often in the list of outcomes experienced by mentees from Part 1. These are the staple diet of many mentoring partnerships.

Professional issues are of concern to many business mentors, who see their role as helping their director mentees focus on matters of direct relevance to the business. Colin Palmer (A8a) and Kees Zandvliet (A13) are cases where professional issues are to the fore.

Technical matters, on the other hand, are not typically issues for mentoring. Coaches or instructors can address these. Technical matters tend to be too specific for the skills and contracts characteristic of mentoring as described in this book.

Again, discussing this framework and deciding where the focus needs to be put are excellent ways of generating a clear contract with the mentee.

Preparation vs. planning

In Richard Field's case (A4) he makes a distinction between preparation and planning. Richard says:

> It is about preparation more than planning. Planning is working backwards from a goal; preparation is like strategy in a business – following the 'plan, do, study, act' cycle. When he was having terrible difficulty setting himself a one-year plan, I asked a friend who was his role model. He said, 'Jesus Christ'. Did Christ plan? No, he prepared.

Richard makes sure that he has 15 minutes of quiet reflection before he meets any of his mentees. This helps him to centre himself and to bring to mind the issues that may be alive for the mentee. Liz Borredon's French informant (A2) had this to say about planning from his point of view as a mentee:

> I realized that if I wanted to benefit from future meetings, I needed to prepare for such meetings, that I come to the meeting with a given subject or subjects about which I want to talk, or specific questions that I have, and to progress in this manner . . . I found that with my degree of preparation the use of the one hour we were limited to was very efficient.

Here he uses the word 'preparation', but it sounds like planning in Richard Field's terms. However, when he takes the role of mentor, sometimes all he can do is Richard's kind of preparation:

> It depends on the meeting. I do sometimes prepare and sometimes I don't. Marc's visits were usually unexpected and so I didn't prepare. I gauged where he was at when he arrived. It is possible to imagine that we are far more advanced than a given person actually is on a given day. We sometimes have to go backwards before moving forward. The pacing and attunement to the individual is important for me.

Ian Flemming, Julia Essex's mentor (B1b) says:

> I prepare for the meetings by having a phone call with Julia on
> what she wants, which I will mull over. Then I offer a plan for
> the meeting, which she may modify.

This indicates both preparation and planning. However, Sir Christopher Ball (C1) reflects on the difference between himself and one of his mentees:

> His plan is much more comprehensive and elaborate than mine,
> with separate sections for himself as a person, family, community
> and work. He turns up to our sessions fully organized, and my
> role is just to ask him, 'Why did that happen?'

Christopher Ball quips that we can follow his own mentor's method and avoid any planning or preparation at all:

> His 'big question' is, 'What did you learn from that, Christopher?'
> I sometimes joke in speeches that, based on my experience of
> Barry, asking this question is all you need to do to be a mentor.

What can we draw from these experiences? We suggest that the mentor's role is to help the mentee to prepare appropriately. What we as mentors need to do is to ready ourselves, reflect on our recent contact with the mentee, and be present to respond to whatever comes up for the mentee when we meet.

Having a process

One of the things we noticed about the most experienced mentors we interviewed was that they seemed to have a process. Often it was an open and flexible process, but nonetheless they had a way of going on. It was also clear that their processes were markedly different for each mentor. So we are not talking here about standardization.

To illustrate this point we give quotations below from five of our interviews:

> I ask them to send me a fax each week saying how they are going
> with the issues that they raised the previous week and anything
> else that concerns them. I fax back to them each Sunday, sending a
> common message from my learning during the week, and also a
> message unique to each of them. I encourage them to look
> holistically at their life and to see if it is in balance; to see what
> they need and if I can support them in that. *Richard Field (A4)*

> I have a process for my work. I start asking about personal
> interests and commitments, and personal goals and vision. Then

I relate this to the business. One of the most useful things up front is to clarify why they are doing this – what their interests and motivations are, and how the business fits into their lives; where they want to be in five or ten years time, and what this means in business terms. It becomes a self-fulfilling prophecy if they keep it in mind. It is also useful to look at where things go out of alignment – especially when working with two people.

I help by reflecting back what they say, by being a role model (having built up a business myself), and by asking good questions – asking the questions behind the questions. So, if two directors of a business say to me that they want to achieve a particular figure for profit next year, I might ask 'Why?' five times, to get back to the fundamental issue. I also end up giving advice on issues of 'protection' and 'exit'. Because I have been there, I talk them through such issues as professional indemnity exposure, registering trade names, preparing for due diligence searches, which require specific advice. *Colin Palmer (A8)*

We started sharing information about each other in terms of Honey & Mumford's learning styles, Myers-Briggs personality styles and also a framework of work styles. *Mike Pupius (A9)*

The initial role is to set the tone and create a climate where both can agree a purpose for the relationship. It is not a cosy role and, while simple in concept, it is complex in practice, evolving uniquely in each case. The relationship is like weaving a Fairisle sweater – looking equally harmonious on both sides, and all the colours fitting with each other. It is a holistic process . . . Every relationship is different, but the mentor is in charge of facilitating the process. Within each meeting, we usually start with a catch-up, where they talk about what they have done since the last meeting. Then I talk for a short time about what has been happening to me, so there is some reciprocity without me using the time to deal with my own issues. Then we identify a theme: 'What would you like today to be about?' We explore what they want from me related to this theme, and then we work upon it. The mentor's job is to attend to this agreement, the purposes, boundaries, processes and benchmarks and to restate them if things go too far off track or become erratic. *Dame Rennie Fritchie (B3)*

. . . follows what I call the 'Ninja Principle': 'Never Interfere; Never Judge or Advise'. *Sir Christopher Ball (C1)*

Challenge and confrontation

Liz Borredon's French director (A2) says:

> ... I think it is the mentor's role to focus enquiry onto one area rather than another. To help the other see other aspects of reality instead of being identified with one single perspective. Alone, we do not see from many perspectives; either we don't see, or we don't want to see. The mentor is not there to be kind or accommodating – the mentor can be confronting, or explicit in saying 'you are avoiding the issue' or 'you have overlooked something and it is important to look into it'.

Three areas that executives can neglect are:

- focus on the business as a whole
- relationships at work
- issues about themselves.

Challenging or confronting questions about each of these areas are listed in Table 3.3.

Table 3.3 Challenging questions for mentors to ask

Business as a whole	Relationships	Themselves
What important issues are you not addressing?	Which relationships are particularly difficult or too comfortable?	What are your current strengths and weaknesses?
What do you miss by focusing on just your own function?	What patterns are there in how you relate to ...?	What knowledge about yourself would you welcome?
What patterns are emerging gradually and are being missed?	Where and how could you improve the effectiveness of the executive team?	How consistent are your values and actions?
How consistent are the business values and how are they applied?	How can you get to hear from people what they are currently unwilling to tell you?	What knowledge about yourself do you avoid?
How can we uncover delusions about strategy and business practice?		What defence mechanism do you put up to avoid self-knowledge?
		How can you discover blocks to your development?
		Could you carry on like this till you retire?
		Do you suffer from vagueness or culpable indecision?

Of course, there are millions of questions that can be asked. These just indicate some of the areas of blindness that have cropped up in the cases we have assembled. Four principles that emerge from the cases, and which can be used when challenging, are:

- Challenge the behaviour not the person.
- Challenge their assumptions not their intellect.
- Challenge their perceptions not their judgement.
- Challenge their values not their value.

Crisis mentoring

We have a number of cases of mentoring in a crisis. The French director (A2) offers an example. It is part of the work of his agency to deal with the crisis of executive redundancy. Nonetheless, the mentor recognizes the limits of his competence:

> ... he was very destabilized by his current situation. I realized that a period of two weeks was far too long for him to wait. So our contract was that Marc could phone me at any moment he needed to, at his initiative, and if I were not in a position to take his call, I would phone him back as soon as I was able. These calls came to my place of work and sometimes to my home ... We were at the limit of a mentoring relationship of the sort we can offer at the VCA; this was a borderline case as he could so easily have required professional psychological help. I took a risk. I was at the limit of my competence but it is not the first time that I had taken such a risk ... The risk of being wrong is almost non-existent as I will not take the person further than I know how. If I know I cannot mentor, I will find the sort of competence that is needed.

Julia Essex (B1b) talks about her various mentors in the following terms:

> I have seen a couple of other people in a sort of mentoring capacity, including an organizational 'bereavement counsellor', provided by an NHS organization, to help deal with a major and unexpected restructuring. They were helpful and specific, but because of my long-term relationship with Ian, I did not need them for long.

However, her long-term mentor could also help in a crisis:

> I got into choppy waters in entering the current job two and a half years ago. Three days before I was due to take up the post, the Chief Executive rang and warned me of an impending restructuring which could imply the removal of the post. I

phoned Ian, who calmed me down and helped me to express my concerns in a positive way. He helped me to handle a very difficult situation positively.

The lessons from these stories are that:

- Mentoring which is set up to deal with crises can do so.
- Normally it should be seen as a long-term intervention.
- Once a high level of trust has been established a long-term mentor can provide valuable support and perspective in a crisis.
- It is crucial that mentors recognize when they are at the limits of their helping capacity and know how to refer people on to others with specialized skills.

Supervision

Supervision in the context of mentoring is the process by which mentors review their cases and gain external support in thinking through the personal and professional dilemmas they face in these relationships. The strongest story of supervision in our cases is that of James Cannon (A3), so we give below quite a long extract to give a flavour of the features of effective supervision:

> ... we decided to follow good practice and appoint an external supervisor for our work. The individual ... was very experienced and each month would work with us in examining our cases and thinking through how to work more effectively with our clients. At some points these became training sessions, whilst at others they took on the character of individual coaching. Overall the relationship was equivalent to that of a mentor. Working as we did as a group and occasionally on a one-to-one basis, it took a little time to build trust both with the mentor and with each other.
>
> In due course, the agenda broadened from looking at just our clients to a range of counselling issues and approaches as well as from time to time looking at the dynamics of our own team.
>
> The supervisor's style was one of persistent questioning interspersed with advice and suggested approaches. Case studies were sometimes used, but invariably we would work from our own experience. His neutrality and gentle manner ensured that he built credibility and trust with everyone ... His many years as a counselling supervisor ensured that he had much relevant experience when called upon to provide an input as well as the skills of probing and reflecting to help us work with the issues.

> Our preparation for each meeting consisted of reviewing our cases of the moment and identifying any which were problematic and needed his input. Certain categories of people, i.e. those who had been with us a long time and were stuck, were automatically brought to the table . . . .
>
> One particularly useful incident came about when I had exhausted everything I could do with a client. The mentor helped me realize that I had done all that was reasonable in the circumstances and another counsellor might bring a fresh perspective. This happened and the client progressed. Without his intervention and the encouragement to let the client go, I might have been tempted to hang on much longer – fearing that to do otherwise might be seen as a failure.

Support of a supervisory kind is valuable for all mentors and, in our view, is essential for professional mentors, because, generally speaking, more is expected of them than of those who do it as an adjunct to their day job. Questions for mentors to ask about supervision include:

*   Where do I go when I feel stuck with someone I am mentoring?
*   What is my worst fear about what might happen with a mentee? What would I do if this seemed to be about to happen?
*   Are my own values and unfulfilled aspirations being laid on my mentee illegitimately?
*   What skills or qualities do I lack as a mentor? Who can help me identify them?
*   How can I compensate for my lack of skill or develop the skills I need?
*   Is dependency developing in the relationship?
*   Do any of my mentees need a change of helper? How would I know?

WIIFM?

The question, 'What's in it for me?' is often asked about executive mentoring, when it is done as a part of another role rather than as a professional mentor. With professional mentors it is clear that mentoring is part of their way of earning a living. However, they also gain many of the satisfactions expressed by part-time mentors, and these benefits are cited in our cases. They include personal rewards, learning rewards and corporate rewards.

Personal rewards include:

*   satisfaction at helping others (generativity, or leaving a legacy)
*   friendship
*   rejuvenation.

Learning benefits include:

- intellectual excitement
- connection to new thinking
- understanding what is happening in parts of the organization to which their seniority makes access difficult
- challenges to their own assumptions
- developing their helping skills.

Corporate rewards include:

- a cadre of committed and well informed younger staff
- successors with strategic vision
- an egalitarian climate where people have significant conversations across layers and functions
- reduced turnover among key executives who are mentored.

Pay and rewards

Only one of our respondents, Sir John Harvey-Jones (A6), advocated rewarding mentors through pay. He says:

> We had numerous people who did not go further in
> management themselves, yet who were absolutely superb in
> developing the right attitudes and aspirations in younger people.
> But we didn't reward them by any other means. They got paid
> for past performance, not for developing the future talent of the
> organization. Now, I would pay a mentor's allowance or find
> some other way of giving greater recognition to the importance
> of what they contribute.

His is a view to be taken seriously, though the matter is important rather than urgent. A great many mentors report intrinsic satisfaction from the activity itself, and, in many contexts this seems to be sufficient to keep them engaged. The alternative view to Sir John's is put by Liz Borredon's *accompagnateur* (A2):

> [M]y client . . . did not trust me, and suspected that I might
> personally exploit the relationship. He did not know what
> motivated me in being a mentor. He wondered why I should
> want to be of help to him, and we had to overcome that
> barrier. We did it through my replying to each question that he
> asked regarding my motives for the relationship. This included
> explaining why I was devoting time and interest in his specific
> company, my interest in him as a professional and an individual,
> and how I felt about the situation. This required a great deal of

> self-disclosure, and we went backwards sometimes as doubt
> crept back in. There were times when I doubted we could
> progress because he was so sceptical and hesitant as to my
> motives. This was a very significant phase. Then there was a
> specific moment when he understood the purpose of the
> relationship and was ready to build on what he had come to
> trust. He saw the role I could play and the help I could offer to
> him in developing his company.

This thoughtful reflection indicates the importance for mentors of being as clear as they can about their own motives for doing this work, and being equally explicit in communicating this to their mentees.

Relationship issues

In the previous two sections we have considered issues that concern predominantly one or other of the mentee and the mentor. In this section we turn to matters where both are equally involved:

* Matching
* Balancing mentoring
* Quality of the relationship
* Frequency and length of meetings
* Review and timescale
* Friendship.

Matching

One way in which we make sense of matching is to consider whether the couple is similar or different with respect to experiences and personality. Figure 3.3 shows four types of relationship that emerge from considering these two dimensions.

The issues for the four types are different. From our cases we can pick out examples of three of them. Not surprisingly, we did not have any stories of unduly *comfortable* relationships.

Nigel Harrison (A8b) has a view of his mentor, Colin Palmer, which emphasizes the *perspective* he offers from his different stance on their shared concerns:

> Colin fits the bill. He has done that with the same sort of
> business that we are in, and what we also like is that he has a
> definite process: as we are process consultants, he does the
> same thing to us that we do to other people. He helps us focus

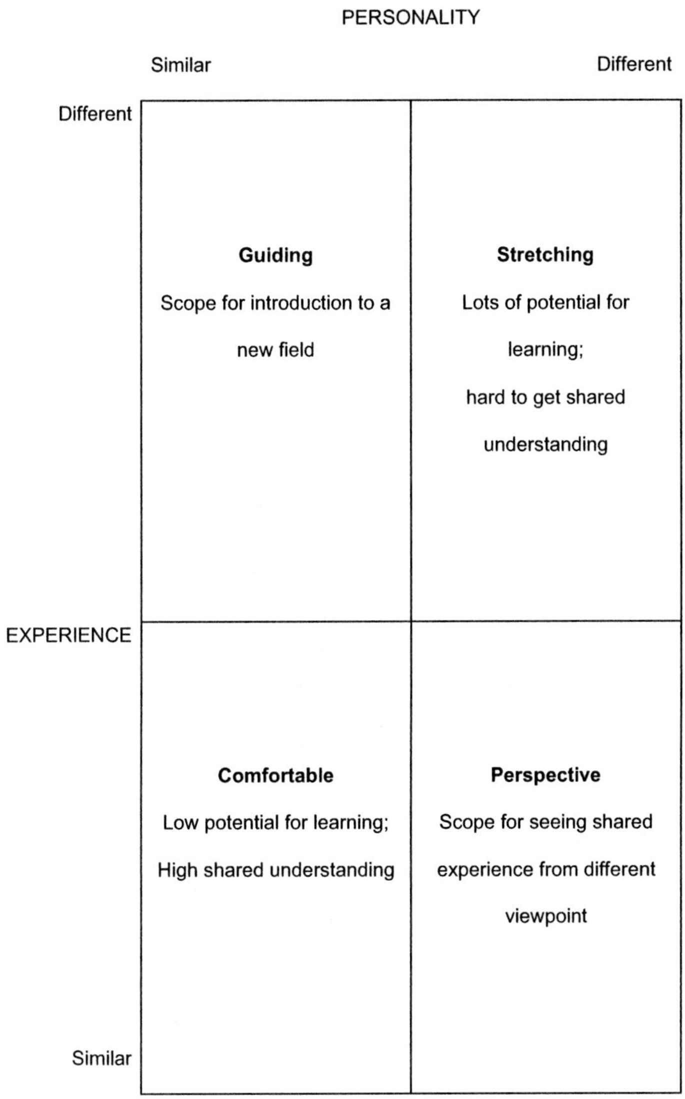

PERSONALITY

Similar   Different

	Similar	Different
Different	**Guiding** Scope for introduction to a new field	**Stretching** Lots of potential for learning; hard to get shared understanding
EXPERIENCE		
Similar	**Comfortable** Low potential for learning; High shared understanding	**Perspective** Scope for seeing shared experience from different viewpoint

Figure 3.3   Types of match in mentoring relationships

> on priority issues. So it is a reflective device for us . . . The way
> that Colin thinks helps us, and the way that he has had contacts
> helps us. So that's very rational and straightforward – and it
> works very well.

David Wilson (B7) experiences his mentor as very different from him,
mainly in terms of his experience. The mentor works for an organization
with a contrasting culture and he has a different role in it. The mentor

can act as a *guide*, which, as this extract shows, does not mean that his suggestions are taken on uncritically:

> We're probably chalk and cheese, and that reflects the teams we work in. I work in a very people-oriented team. He works in an organization that places a lot of value on systems, processes and paper. It is an interesting tension. When I talk about the way we do things here, how we achieve results, he suggests a totally different perspective – a view that forces me to think and evaluate why I am doing and saying things in my current way. There is a tension, but both of us know that neither has the complete answer. It's not that sort of relationship. I'm not asking the 'what' and 'how' questions expecting direct answers. It's more about mutual exploration and suspending judgement.

Philip Lewer (B5) offers a case of maximum *stretching*, and indicates that it takes a lot of effort to make such relationships work:

> I see my mentors as being totally different from me . . . Relationships that have worked have started informally – I have been impelled to seek something by an awareness of my own lack of something. At the start I have had fears of exposing too much of myself and being vulnerable, but as the relationship gets more established these fears disappear.

On matching, Rennie Fritchie (B3) suggests: 'There are no rules about whether mentor and mentee should be similar or different. They could be either, so long as you know which it is.' As with so much about executive mentoring, consciousness of the issues, and readiness to address them in partnership, are what most matters.

Trude Stolpe (A11) indicates how this insight was achieved in the case of her company Axel Johnsson:

> Mentors were given a self-assessment questionnaire to provide a profile, against which mentees could select. Mentees were given a questionnaire to help them define what sort of person they were looking for, then a set of mentor profiles. The mentees were then responsible for informing the mentor of their choice.

A message from this experience seems to be that, whether you are thinking about a scheme or an individual relationship, it is important to maximize the choice for mentees.

Balancing mentoring
In the account of Sir Christopher Ball's mentoring (C1) he places a huge emphasis on learning and also discusses personal exploration and life

balance. On the other hand, Julia Essex (B1a) talks principally about work performance and career. Is there a right list? We do not think so. We do think, however, that it is important to reflect on what the issues are that you want to address, both as mentor and mentee.

One way of structuring this reflection is to imagine that you have 100 points to distribute between a number of issues. At the start of a relationship the mentor might like to discuss with the mentee what are the issues that the mentee wants to address and how they might distribute the 100 points among these issues. Then after a time both could review in their opinion how the points were being distributed in the relationship currently, and the mentee could propose how they would like them to be distributed in the future.

To illustrate, take an example of a director interested in learning as a main aim of their being mentored. A notional example of how the points might be distributed is shown in Table 3.4. Their desired mix at the start might have been as in Column A. At the review, the mentor might have seen it as in Column B, with the mentee's view of how it is shown in Column C and their view of how they would like it to be in Column D.

Table 3.4 Example of the balance of emphasis on issues during a mentoring relationship

Issue	A Mentee at start	B Mentor now	C Mentee now	D Mentee wish
Learning	50	60	55	50
Personal exploration	20	15	5	10
Balance of life	5	10	10	10
Relationships	10	5	10	5
Performance	5	0	10	5
Career	5	5	5	15
Business development	5	5	5	5

These figures could provide a jumping-off point for a review of the relationship, with the mentee making it clear what changes, if any, they would like to see in how the relationship might progress. The mentee could respond with suggestions about what would make sense for them. In this case the reasons for the difference in perception about the emphasis placed on 'Personal exploration' could be examined and the need for more attention to 'Career' would seem to be a priority for discussion.

Whether or not you want to prepare a table or specify percentages, the principle of looking at the balance of the relationship and how it is evolving over time can be a useful one. The list of issues in the table above is just an example and there are many others that you may wish to include, for example:

- major transitions
- director's role
- significant projects
- health/stress/use of stimulants.

Our advice is to create your own list, or at any rate have a conversation about what priorities are and how they are changing.

Qualities of the relationship

Our director co-researchers noticed the following issues in the cases they examined:

- Relationships were often triggered when the mentee was in a crisis, and they were often re-activated by subsequent crises.
- The mentor entered into the relationship with the expectation that it might be long-term rather than just for a fixed period, although emphasis was placed on the importance of having a means to come to a good conclusion if this seemed appropriate.
- Trust was a crucial dimension in the relationship.
- Overcoming isolation was a key consequence of the relationship.
- It was important for the chemistry to be right and the partners were well able to judge whether this was the case.
- Mutual respect was a critical precursor of success in executive mentoring relationships.
- Preparation by both parties and, to a lesser extent, planning by the mentee, before the meetings helped.

Frequency and length of meetings

Mentoring is a powerful intervention, but it is not magic. For it to work there needs to be sufficient time spent for a relationship to be established and issues to be explored. Among our respondents Richard Field (A4), with his weekly fax contact, was the most frequent. Liz Borredon's French director (A2) also had a short time between meetings, because the work was being done with newly redundant unemployed senior managers, so there was some considerable urgency. More typically, mentoring of senior managers takes place at intervals of one to three months and for periods of two to three hours on each occasion. There is often telephone or e-mail contact in between. For company schemes it is helpful, as they did at ABB

(A5), to set a norm (in their case 10–12 meetings a year). Otherwise mentoring can wither on the vine before its roots penetrate deep enough to become self-sustaining.

Review and timescale

Richard Hale, whose account of David Wilson's experience of mentoring is included in Part 2 (B7), has produced a review format that can be used by mentor and mentee to examine their relationship. It can be obtained from him at the International Management Centres, 13 Castle Street, Buckingham, Bucks, England (tel: 01280–817222; fax: 01280–813297). Other formats for the same purpose are available from the European Mentoring Centre, Burnham House, Burnham, Bucks, England. Whether you use such a form, create a customized one or use no form at all, there is a strong case for doing a periodic review of all mentoring relationships.

Liz Borredon's respondent says:

> At the end of the year each of us, separately, evaluated the period. I did this in writing. I was not given a form and this was not imposed but I wanted to reflect on the year and I thought that writing was the best way to do so. So I wrote down what I thought the relationship had given me, whether it met my expectations, and if so, whether this person would be able to help me in what I hoped to achieve, or in the programme I had set myself for the following year.

There is nearly always something surprising to learn from a conscious review of a relationship, however open and frank the relationship has been. A suggested frequency for such a review would be every six or so meetings, although any sign of dissatisfaction with the relationship from either party is the primary indicator that it is time to review.

On the question of the overall timescale of the relationship, Richard Field (A4) says there should be no limits:

> Nor do I have any timescale for the mentoring – it is like family: I am part of their path for however long it takes.

In Julia Essex's case (B1a), her mentor has persisted for more than six years while she has held jobs in three different organizations:

> You get the greatest benefit from a long-term relationship because this becomes increasingly effective as you do not have to keep re-explaining things.

Others make a case for very definite boundaries, though with the opportunity for extension. For example, Liz Borredon's French director (A2) reports:

> After the first year, the relationship ended officially. I was told
> we would both evaluate the year together, and then, if
> appropriate a new year could be initiated with the same person,
> or I could ask for another mentor.

The use of boundaries to bring issues to the fore and to re-evaluate what
has been achieved is certainly a strong argument for having a fixed
period. It also facilitates the ending of relationships in a no-blame way.
However, some mentors thrive on developing a relationship that merges
progressively into friendship, and this is a legitimate alternative model.
It is to the subject of friendship that we now turn.

Friendship

Mentoring is one of the most intense forms of development that we know
of. It can evoke strong feelings both for the people involved and those
looking on from the outside. Reports of sexual jealousy on the part of
observers are not uncommon, for example from Trude Stolpe's account
(A11):

> One relationship involved a very beautiful woman and a 55-year-
> old man. There was a lot of negative comment and
> misconceptions when they met in the evening. It was an issue
> that participants really needed to think about.

However, the precious flower of friendship could bloom in a mentoring
relationship that achieves any kind of depth, where the parties come to
care about each other. The question is, should it? Liz Borredon's French
respondent (A2) makes the case against:

> . . . it is important to maintain a certain distance in order to
> help the person conclude what they have to do.

Rennie Fritchie (B3), who is as engaged and engaging a mentor as you
could hope to meet, also cautions against confusing the relationship with
friendship:

> She seemed jolly and outgoing, but when I asked her what her
> goals were for the mentoring she included my 'being her friend'.
> I find this is not a part of the professional relationship of
> mentoring – especially if it is being paid for. With friends both
> parties take time to deal with their own matters. In this
> relationship she became very needy, and I felt overwhelmed after
> our sessions. She wanted advice, connections, friendship, therapy,
> a mother. I decided to let the relationship go.

Others, such as Ian Flemming (B1b) report a measure of friendliness:

> My relationship with Julia is both formal and informal. It is
> formal in the sense of my trying to get some clarity from her
> about what her agenda is before she arrives. It is also paid, and
> we work to strict time boundaries. It also has informal qualities,
> as we are friendly, and I like her.

A similar ambivalence is expressed by Philip Lewer (B5), who says of one of his mentors:

> I speak to her over the phone once a week and see her
> perhaps once a month. On these occasions we sometimes have
> a drink together. The relationship is bordering upon friendship, in
> a way that the other two are not.

Richard Field (A4) is not ambivalent about this matter:

> A mentor is a friend, a coach, a judge and an encourager. You
> have got to have enormous trust and a long-term relationship –
> which can be created in moments. To do this you have to be
> prepared to be totally vulnerable – when I have given trust, I
> don't think I have ever been let down.

On the one hand there is a keeping of professional boundaries, on the other a modelling of single-minded commitment. Those of us who mentor are faced with a choice in this matter and, as in so much about this engaging subject, there are no easy right answers. The way forward is to do what you do to be your kind of mentor, with conscious awareness, and with the humility to check that it is working for the others involved.

Endnote

John Ruskin (1856) says:

> The greatest thing a human soul ever does in this world is to
> see something, and to tell what it saw in a plain way. Hundreds
> of people can talk for one who can think, but thousands can
> think for one who can see. To see clearly is poetry, prophecy
> and religion – all in one.

This is not a bad touchstone for the role of the mentor.

References

Argyris, C. (1993) *Knowledge in Action*. San Francisco: Jossey-Bass.

Caruso, R. (1996) Who does mentoring? The pursuit of the dream. In D. Megginson and D. Clutterbuck (1996) *Proceedings of the Third European Mentoring Conference*. EMC, Burnham House, Burnham, Bucks. pp. 67–76.

Casey, D. (1993) *Learning in Organisations*. Milton Keynes: Open University Press.

Clutterbuck, D. (1998) *Learning Alliances*. London: Institute of Personnel & Development.

Clutterbuck, D. (1993) *Mentoring at Oxford Regional Health Authority: A Project Appraisal*. Burnham: DCA.

Clutterbuck, D. and Devine, M. (eds) (1987) *Businesswoman*. Basingstoke: Macmillan.

Garratt, B. (1996) *The Fish Rots From the Head*. London: HarperCollins.

Goldsmith, W. and Clutterbuck, D. (1997) *The Winning Streak Mark II*. London: Orion.

Goleman, D. (1996) *Emotional Intelligence*. London: Bloomsbury.

Levinson, D. (1978) *The Seasons of a Man's Life*. New York: Alfred Knopf.

Megginson, D. and Clutterbuck, D. (1995) *Mentoring in Action*. London: Kogan Page.

Megginson, D. and Clutterbuck, D. (eds) (1998) *Proceedings of the Fifth European Mentoring Conference*. EMC, Burnham House, Burnham, Bucks.

Munford, A., Honey, P. and Robinson, G. (1990) *Director's Development Guidebook: Making Experience Count*. London: Director Publications.

Ruskin, J. (1856) *Modern Painters*. Works, Library Edition, Volume V.

Willcox, T. (1987) Mentoring among British executives, Part 1: the British case. *Int. J. Mentoring*, **1**(1), 19–23.

Index

Printed in the United Kingdom
by Lightning Source UK Ltd.
101737UKS00003BC/29-36